Dark Justice

It is difficult to imagine a more heinous crime than the sexual abuse of children. Yet, terrifyingly, a new case of child sexual abuse is reported every seven minutes. In response to this crisis, self-appointed groups of citizens are fashioning themselves as 'paedophile hunters'. Operating outside the law, these groups use social media to bait and expose those seeking to engage children sexually, both on- and offline. Their work has been remarkably effective, but at what cost? Following four years of unprecedented access to the UK's most prolific team of paedophile hunters, Mark de Rond offers balanced and insightful answers to the perplexing question of why these groups persist in using extreme methods to hold predators to account in view of less harmful alternatives. In doing so, he invites us to consider the societal impacts of paedophile hunters on our laws and institutions, as well as societal cohesion and safety.

Mark de Rond is Professor of Organisational Ethnography at Cambridge Judge Business School. He immerses himself in the lives of his subjects, who have included doctors and nurses at war in Afghanistan, a ragtag band rowing the length of the river Amazon, Boat Race crews and paedophile hunters. In his work, he seeks to engage with questions to which the answers can actually make a positive difference to real people in really challenging situations.

'*Dark Justice* is an ethnographic barnburner, a moral bombshell and a narrative page-turner all rolled into one. It will make you revise all your cherished beliefs about evil, justice and citizenship in the age of out-of-control social media.'
Loïc Wacquant, author of *Body and Soul: Notebooks of an Apprentice Boxer* and *Punishing the Poor*

'Mark de Rond may be the best writer in social science today. His book on paedophile hunters grabs your attention from the first line. He is also one of the most intrepid practitioners of deep ethnography. He describes a world full of dangers – violent, criminal-legal and moral – where the wrongs are emphatic but doing something about them risks even more wrongs. The moral ambiguities of today's world of interaction by internet are here clearly on display.'
Randall Collins, author of *Explosive Conflict: Time-Dynamics of Violence*

'This book is incredible! In *Dark Justice* Mark de Rond tells a gripping account of his time with a group of citizens who take it upon themselves to hunt online child predators. Writing like a novelist with his stream-of-consciousness style, he delivers an unflinching examination of what motivates people to personally fight child exploitation. Through a narrative of personal reflections and nail-biting firsthand accounts, *Dark Justice is* a compelling, deeply moving account that lays bare the complexities and ethical quandaries faced by those who pursue predators in their quest for safeguarding innocence.'
Katy DeCelles, Inaugural VMWare Women's Leadership Innovation Lab Fellow

'Mark de Rond's newest book provides important insight into the work of vigilantes who track and entrap paedophiles. Embedded for years on paedophile hunting teams, de Rond's compelling storytelling explores the many narratives of these hunters including their tenuous relationship with police forces. He forces us to rethink our own relationship with the justice system as we seek to make sense of its grievous failures in protecting children from the most abhorrent crimes. de Rond's work pushes us to engage in broader conversations around citizen activism and accountability as we absorb a brilliant and uncomfortable look into the largely invisible work done by paedophile hunters.'

Tina Dacin, Professor and Stephen J. R. Smith
Chair of Strategy and Organizational Behaviour,
Queen's University

'*Dark Justice* is a deeply insightful and important exploration of a morally ambiguous world, one wherein the desire of small citizen activated groups to protect innocent children from harm collide with the duplicitous scripts they follow to stamp out predatorial behaviour. A personal and reflexive ethnography that holds little back, recounting the grim and troubling activities of UK and Scotland hunters and decoys as well as their targets. Deftly written around the captivating but nuanced accounts of varied encounters – 'stings' – taking place in the enigmatic sphere of identifying and tracking down paedophiles. A treatment of the good, the bad and the ugly as told by a compassionate narrator who draws on four years of participant observation with several groups deemed successful at what they do as well as knowledgeable police officials familiar with the domain and types of encounters inscribed. This vivid narrative is something of a shadow parable for our internet age since so much of the activities of the hunters and their prey relies on social media.'

John Van Maanen, author of *Tales of the Field*

Dark Justice
Inside the World of Paedophile Hunters

Mark de Rond

CAMBRIDGE
UNIVERSITY PRESS

CAMBRIDGE
UNIVERSITY PRESS

Shaftesbury Road, Cambridge CB2 8EA, United Kingdom

One Liberty Plaza, 20th Floor, New York, NY 10006, USA

477 Williamstown Road, Port Melbourne, VIC 3207, Australia

314–321, 3rd Floor, Plot 3, Splendor Forum, Jasola District Centre, New Delhi – 110025, India

103 Penang Road, #05–06/07, Visioncrest Commercial, Singapore 238467

Cambridge University Press is part of Cambridge University Press & Assessment, a department of the University of Cambridge.

We share the University's mission to contribute to society through the pursuit of education, learning and research at the highest international levels of excellence.

www.cambridge.org
Information on this title: www.cambridge.org/9781009457040

DOI: 10.1017/9781009457026

First published 2025

Printed in the United Kingdom by CPI Group Ltd, Croydon CR0 4YY

A catalogue record for this publication is available from the British Library.

A Cataloging-in-Publication data record for this book is available from the Library of Congress.

ISBN 978-1-009-45704-0 Hardback

CONTENTS

On the Title of This Book   ix

Chapter 1   1

Chapter 2   8

Chapter 3   20

Chapter 4   24

Chapter 5   33

Chapter 6   38

Chapter 7   50

Chapter 8   54

Chapter 9   64

Chapter 10   69

Chapter 11   77

Chapter 12   82

Chapter 13   89

Chapter 14   92

Chapter 15   101

Chapter 16   107

Chapter 17   109

Chapter 18   134

Chapter 19   145

Chapter 20   152

Epilogue   153

Appendix: Notes on Methodology   158
When They Read What We Write   165
Acknowledgements   178
Notes   180

ON THE TITLE OF THIS BOOK

There once was a paedophile hunting team called Dark Justice, but this book isn't about them.

Even so, I did always think Scott and Callum (its co-founders) admirable. Their evidence was repeatedly used in court to convict paedophiles and keep our children much safer than they otherwise would have been. I was as sorry as many others when Scott announced Callum had died in a tragic accident.

To anyone who's ever stood up for somebody else

1

I work hard to make myself invisible – a pair of jeans and old sneakers, a black sweatshirt and jacket, a woollen hat and Buff scarf – but the Harry Potter specs let me down. I've not got another pair. *Jesus.* I tell Jay. He smiles and says he was going to put me in 'uniform' anyways and tosses me a zipless grey hoodie. It has COBRA's snakehead logo and CHILDREN ONLINE BATTLING REAL ABUSE in large letters on the back. Explains our presence to local gangs, he says, who may otherwise take us for rival hoodlums. His wife, Saz, smokes non-stop. Our destination is a shithole.

'That's a lot of masturbating right there,' Jay says as he gestures at his 'paedo-pack' in the backseat. 'There's four DVDs in here with 20GBs of evidence and printouts of all the correspondence between the suspect and the hundred kids he "pulled in" to watch him doing it on Facebook.'

Saz tells me they handed this evidence to the police months ago, but the police never acted on it. 'Something isn't right about this predator,' Saz says, 'but police don't say what it is.' What they did tell us is not to 'sting' tonight's suspect because if we do, *we* will get arrested instead. It is why Jay will hold tight to his 'paedo-pack' seeing as we may need to do a runner.

Saz shows me a screenshot of the suspect's face. He looks young and Mediterranean. Has she told other team members that I'm there only to observe? I ask. Yes, she says and tells me not to worry;

that she's told their security detail to keep an eye out for me 'so he knows to protect ya, just encase'.

Too anxious to do any serious academic work in the hours before meeting up with Jay and Saz, I scoured recent news coverage of paedophile hunting instead. I read about the suffering of families who were as stunned as anyone to discover what was happening under their roofs. I read about suicides following public spectacles of humiliation. What I didn't know was that at least one of these would be happening on my watch and nor that they follow an upward trajectory, from a dozen suicides between 2017 and 2020 to seven in 2022, and ten in 2023, not counting any unsuccessful attempts.[1] I read about cases of mistaken identity; about the suspect who bit the tip of a hunter's finger clean off. About how hunters themselves are vulnerable to attacks online and know it. About how they use Article 24a[2] of the Police and Criminal Evidence Act to justify a 'citizen's arrest' (a term that has formally been replaced by 'arrestable offence') and often do so inappropriately.

I read about a predator avenging himself on the hunter who exposed him by telling the police that she posts home-videos of herself abusing her own children, and so why not arrest her instead. So, the police came knocking one afternoon. She said the sight of the police at her door made her sick to her stomach and she barely made it to the toilet. Did the police not know that the predator had sworn to exact revenge on her, and that this is what revenge in the hunting community looks like?

I read about a survivor of abuse who'd helped to convict twenty-eight paedophiles only to discover a doctored photo that showed him calling for a lowering of the age of consent to 6 years of age. I looked at the photo. Frankly, the doctoring looked like a botched job: a slogan saying 'paedophiles are people' had been photoshopped onto a placard that originally said much the opposite. But the damage was done. Using Twitter, trolls called for the hunter to be hanged for his sins. In response to complaints, Twitter merely said that the trolls' actions hadn't constituted a violation of rules against abusive behaviour, so there.[3]

I wrote an email to the dean of my university department and also to my police contact, warning them not to be surprised if I ever fell foul of similar tactics and telling them I'd be out with hunters for the foreseeable future. The police were quick to reply, wishing me good luck and reminding me that I have their number should I feel the need to debrief anything I witness. My dean told me I'm crazy.

I cracked open the window ever so slightly as I drove to the small town where Jay and Saz told me they live. I hadn't been given an address and, after an hour of driving, pulled off the road to text Jay for directions. I figured that information would be dispensed on an as-needed basis and so bided my time, tuning the radio into a comedy programme to take the edge off. Half an hour later, I pulled into a suburban cul-de-sac to see Jay rummaging in the boot of his hatchback. He gave me the biggest smile and why not get in the backseat of their car?

During our drive they brief me on what will happen on arrival in London.

JAY HUNTER

I'll knock on the door and tell him that we're from a childhood protection team and is there any chance he could step outside so we can have a chat. At that point people usually go into shock and so that leaves you with a couple of minutes to do whatever you want to do, and once they start talking the real shock comes when they suddenly realise that we're not police. I will ask him if it's okay if I link arms with him and that the guy on the other side links arms with him, and so when we get their permission, and then we've got an arm each and he's not going anywhere. If he says no and gets agitated, then obviously we won't grab him by the arms but what we do is have me stand in front and Vince, our head of security, behind him, so they've got a bit of an obstacle in case they do a runner –

SAZ DECOY

When it's my turn I tell him that I am going to be filming him and if they start becoming agitated, I just reassure them that no harm is being done to them. And then I say, 'You will be arrested,' and I know the others take the mickey of me because I get predators to look at my face because while they're concentrating on me, they're not concentrating on anyone else, and so I keep telling him to 'look at my face, look at my face' –

JAY HUNTER
Tonight will be live streamed –

SAZ DECOY
Because police have done nothing for four months, but they've threatened to arrest us and so we're putting this out to the public because it's disgusting –

JAY HUNTER
And if they do decide to arrest me it's all out in the public domain and so we've got Vince to live stream my arrest –

SAZ DECOY
We call him the Facebook Flasher. They all get names because that's how you remember them. It's not the nudity that gets you. It's what they say they want to do to a child. And some things of the things they say they want to do; it makes your stomach churn –

JAY HUNTER
Remember that bloke we caught in Deptford?

SAZ DECOY
We got given the sting and I read it and, I'm not gonna lie, I was like, really? We're going out for this? But Jay said, a chat's a chat and so we arranged to go and pick him up at his house. The boys went up to the door and there was an old lady there who was his mother and said he was out with his wife in the town. We didn't want to wait for him to come back to the house because of how old she was, and we wasn't going to give her a heart attack or anything, and so we agreed to go into town and try and find him there. And so we saw him shopping in town, and so the boys approached him, and I took his wife to one side, and then while we were interviewing him, he actually admitted that he is a paedophile, that he's been doing it for many years. He said he was in a ring and named all the other people in the ring –

JAY HUNTER

Then, when the police came, they said that the chat logs don't look much, and so I said that he's just admitted everything in a live stream, and that said he's in a ring –

SAZ DECOY

They released him the next morning. The detective laughed at me and said there's no real kids involved, and I said, 'Are you for real?' and then the detective told us he confessed because he was intimidated. I said, 'You clearly haven't watched the video, have you?' I said 'I want you to re-arrest him, and you have 48 hours before I put this out live'–

JAY HUNTER

So we put it online –

SAZ DECOY

I did give them an extra twenty-four hours just in case and put a warning on there to say this is upsetting because for people that are survivors, they was reliving what was happening to them. We were apologising that we had to put this out but if police do nothing, what do you do?

JAY HUNTER

As far as predators are concerned, they're talking to real children –

Tonight's predator has a particular compulsion: he likes being watched by kids while knocking one off and has been at it for over 300 consecutive days. Jay and Saz tell me of another predator like that, who filmed himself 'at it' with vegetables. Because of this, the decoy no longer eats vegetables and refuses to go down the vegetable aisle when food shopping.

'Fucking idiot,' says Jay, who's had to view all sixty-four videos in putting together the evidence pack.

Having left our car in the parking lot of a supermarket, we walk into a nearby housing estate. Jay tells us to stay out of sight as he and Vince walk up to one of the apartment buildings and press the suspect's bell. When no one answers, they push every single button on the intercom until told by one irate occupant that the suspect isn't at home and, no, he hasn't seen him around for a while now and, no, he doesn't have any idea where he could be, and could they please go away.

Not one to give up easily, Jay uses a trick of the trade: he phones the suspect pretending to be a package delivery driver needing to confirm an address. But the predator tells him he doesn't remember ordering anything and hangs up. So Jay texts him to say that the package will be sent back to the warehouse if he does not confirm his address. Jay says that the predator is onto us, and so the hunt is on.

'His brother was arrested a few weeks ago,' Jay says, 'and done for weapons possession and so our predator doesn't want to be found.' To hear that the brother has also been picked up is news to me if not quite the surprise I thought it would be to the rest of the team. They have long suspected that predators' families are often implicated beyond what they let on.

Jay meanwhile has other tricks up his sleeve and suggests we head back to the car for a sandwich and Red Bull and for him to talk us through Plan B. The popularity of VPNs had made it difficult to locate suspects, Saz says, but that there are no limits to how ingenious hunters are. Once, she says, they identified a suspect's location by way of two distinctive trees that were in a photograph by the predator posted online and, on the satellite version of Google Maps, had looked just as distinctive. On another occasion, they wore hi-vis jackets and marked off a bit of road and pretended to start roadworks while doing reconnaissance in a neighbourhood they were sure contained the suspect. On yet another they told everyone they were following up on an insurance claim for a road traffic accident and going door-to-door asking if anyone knew where a certain so-and-so lived. It is how we once ended up with a wife ratting out her husband, who happened to be watching TV in the living room behind her. The point is that they will do what it takes to get predators off the streets, Saz says, 'so they can harm no children no more'. She tells me all this as we walk back to the car.

Plan B involves a night drive across London to an address where, Jay says, the parents of the suspect's girlfriend live. There isn't much to be gained by trying the suspect's parents seeing they may be in on it, and so Jay figures we might as well aim for the girlfriend's family instead. Even if it means coming up empty-handed, her parents will want to know what their daughter's boyfriend has been up to. And so, an hour later, Jay and Vince knock on the door of an end-of-terrace in a neighbourhood like any other.

When a middle-aged man opens the door at last it's red faces all around. The woman we are here to protect isn't a young girl but the man's elderly mum, and no, she doesn't have a boyfriend, and yes, her last name is a common one in Greece, and no, he doesn't think it okay to take one's chances and turn up unannounced. To have found two women sharing the same name in a city of nine million isn't quite the discovery Jay had hoped it to be.

Police meanwhile are 'blue lighting' the neighbourhood. Jay, Saz, Vince and the rest of the team make their escape to regroup a few minutes later for smokes on a nearby street corner. No one is in a hurry to go home even though it is now midnight, and they all know it will take at least another couple of hours to get home. Police do a couple of drive-bys and, at one point, slow down for a closer look. One of the hunters makes a half-turn away from the road and towards a garden wall. 'Can't afford to be seen by the Old Bill,' he says.

2

It is hard to conjure up something more universally abhorrent than adults grooming children into doing what they are too young to understand but old enough to remember. Yet it is widespread. UK police are given one new child abuse claim to investigate every seven minutes[1] while child protective services in the US substantiate a claim of sexual abuse every nine minutes.[2] The National Crime Agency (NCA) estimates that 550,000 to 850,000 people pose a sexual threat to children in the UK today. Together with the police the NCA arrests, on average, 842 of these every month while also safeguarding 1,092 children.[3,4] The Independent Inquiry into Child Sexual Abuse offers some insight into how this divides up into gender and socio-economic circumstance: girls are at least three times as likely as boys to report abuse;[5] disabled participants twice as likely as abled ones; and those who lived in a care home nearly four times as likely.[6] It highlights the vulnerabilities that predators are most likely to exploit: being in care, experiencing episodes of going missing, and learning disabilities. There is no single factor indicating that any particular group of children is uniquely vulnerable.[7] But of course having been abused does not also mean owning up to the abuse: the FBI and Justice Department suspect that only one in every ten cases is actually reported.[8] Beyond the US and UK, estimates of child sexual abuse globally suggest that one in five girls will be abused before turning 18. For boys this number is one in eleven. Other estimates are more pessimistic yet: 25 to 38 per cent of girls and 17 to 25 per cent of boys suffer sexual abuse. According to the US Department of Health and Human Services, children who live with the unemployed or are from low-income households are twice as likely to be abused, while those who live with a stepparent or live-in partner are twenty times more likely to become victims.[9,10] For those living in the countryside, and for whatever reason, the risks are twice as high.[11]

This then is a short chapter about numbers.

A 2001 study by the US Department of Justice found that 19 per cent of girls had received a 'sexual solicitation' online.[12] A closer look at the numbers suggests that half of all these solicitations had been sent by other teenagers and none led to sexual assault. In fact, aggressive solicitation by adults accounted for 'only' 3 per cent of cases.[13] The Department also suggested that reported cases of child sexual abuse had declined from a peak of 149,800 cases in 1992 to 103,600 cases in 1998 (or a reduction of 31 per cent). Whether this trend continues today isn't clear, and nor is it clear what explains it. One possible explanation is a real underlying decline in the incidence of child sexual abuse; another is changes in attitudes or policies.[14] It could be that fewer cases of child sexual abuse are being reported and substantiated.[15] Given that these data precede the age of social media, it seems reasonable to expect the data to disproportionally reflect 'contact' abuse, involving, as has long been suspected, abusers well known to the victim or victim's family.

Social media has been something of a boon for those hooked on child sexual imagery, much of which is now generated by children in the privacy of their own bedrooms. Children do so at the encouragement of predators posing as fans, and often in exchange for gift tokens or TikTok unicorns or whichever means of exchange happens to be profitable for social media platforms, seeing how little of it is converted back into real money. WhatsApp, Facebook, Meet24, Jaumo, Snapchat, Kik and Grindr are the most popular of at least sixty-five platforms identified by the police as having been used for grooming.

Where gift-giving fails, blackmail makes for a popular alternative. As one witness told the Independent Inquiry, when she tried to cut off her online predator, 'he threatened to screenshot our messages and show everyone how disgusting I was for seeing the things he'd sent'. Another witness said that things were fine so long as she played along, 'but if I ever pushed back the threats got worse. It was a never-ending spiral as he had worse and worse pictures of me.'[16] Here too the figures are bewildering. During 2021 alone, tech companies identified 46 million unique photos and videos featuring child sexual abuse, or a number double that of the previous year, many of which can be accessed in just three 'clicks'. Covid-induced lockdowns fuelled this increase as well as raising the demand for more younger performers (55 per cent of child porn today features children aged 10 or under[17]) and ever more extreme imagery. That this count includes only newly created images leaves one to guess just how many pictures are in circulation today.

The cost of this abuse is not just psychological. A Home Office study estimated the economic cost of abuse to the UK at more than £10 billion.[18] When other forms of child abuse are included – children forced to work in hazardous conditions, for example, and those forced into conscription by militias – the price tag globally (based on the estimated average lifetime cost per victim, including health care costs and productivity loss) is thought to be $7 trillion.[19,20] Target 16.2 of the United Nations Sustainable Development Goals specifically calls on all countries to 'end abuse, exploitation, trafficking and all forms of violence against, and torture of, children' by 2030. Thirty-four countries who responded to a 2017 survey by the Organisation for Economic Co-operation and Development (OECD) reported to have already adopted new laws, policies and education initiatives aimed at protecting children online.

Unsettling though these estimates are, they won't likely hold our attention for as long as stories of abuse headlining the news: Jeffrey Epstein and his 'Lolita Express' to 'Orgy Island' is a particularly well-known example. But there are others too who, like him, abused their power: Jimmy Savile, Max Clifford, Sidney Cooke, Gary Glitter, Rolf Harris, Ian Watkins, grooming gangs in Rochdale, Rotherham and Huddersfield (UK), MS-13 and similar sex trafficking gangs in the US and elsewhere,[21] not to mention clergy, youth leaders, teachers, doctors and others with easy access to children. Where cases are shrouded in allegations of cover-ups and failures by the police, these fuel suspicions that lawmakers, the judiciary and police are incapable of, or uninterested in, keeping children safe; that they are asleep at the wheel or 'in on it'.[22,23,24] Such widespread distrust has led some to take grievances to the streets and matters into their own hands. Others, like me, decide to go along for the ride.

Citizen activism isn't of course a new phenomenon. A big difference today is that social media has significantly lowered the threshold to bait, trace and expose those who prey on children online. It also offers the ability to efficiently coordinate with others without needing to be in the same physical space, and to appeal directly to the public for a mandate to do more of the same. Social media is also without equal in enabling the punishment of moral infractions by public humiliation.[25,26] The template adopted by paedophile hunting teams in the US and UK mimics that of the Dateline NBC series *To Catch a Predator*, where adult members of Perverted Justice (a paedophile hunting group) pretended to be 13- or 14-year-olds online waiting to be approached by men with a sexual interest in children.[27] The series ran for twelve episodes, each one set in a 'sting house' in a different jurisdiction. Men were persuaded to travel long distances to meet the girl or boy they'd been talking to online and, once made to feel at ease, would see their 'child' disappear into an adjacent room to make space for Chris Hansen, host of the show. Hansen typically began his interrogation with a disarming 'what's going on?' before dialling up the entertainment by reading out salacious snaps from the online chat.[28] As if this undressing wasn't sufficiently embarrassing, Hansen then tells the predator that he'll shortly be 'on air', one of several showcases on Dateline. As the predator takes his leave in a great hurry, he is met, cuffed and arrested by America's finest, who followed all proceedings via remote camera from a windowless U-Haul truck parked nearby.

To Catch a Predator was widely criticised for 'entrapment' in facilitating the construction of an online fantasy to goad men into ever more explicit conversations. Many were persuaded to visit their 'child' at the decoy house. The thing is, because sexual communication with a child itself is sufficient grounds for arrest and conviction, there was never a legal need to lure predators into meeting their 'child' except to provide entertainment. Moreover, research shows that the decoys used by Dateline didn't always do a good job at mimicking children's behaviour online: real kids are far more likely to cease communications with predators than decoys are.[29] Perverted Justice, who decoyed for Dateline, encouraged men in ways that real children are unlikely to, as is evident from excerpts from chat logs:

johnchess2000: *anything you want me to wear or bring?*

AJ's Girl: *hmm*

johnchess2000: *wow your thinking for a long time*

AJ's Girl: *sowwy*

AJ's Girl: *u better bring condoms*

johnchess2000: *wow. Condoms??*

Here's another one:

jteno72960: *i love to kiss*

katiedidsings: *me 2*

jteno72960: *really what else*

katiedidsings: *i dunno watevr u wantd 2 do*

jteno72960: *well what have u done*

katiedidsings: *evry thing*

katiedidsings: *wel not evrything*

katiedidsings: *but alot of stuff*

jteno72960: *well what did u like*

katiedidsings: *from behind*

It stretches credulity that a real child would respond as warmly to solicitation or be as forthright in matters of personal preference. Where predators were slow to make a move, Perverted Justice's decoys offered encouragement:

rkline05: *idk i just wasnt sure you wanted to you are a virgin and all*

rkline05: *you sure you want it to be me that takes that*

shyshiagirl: *yea why not. ur cool*

rkline05: *[. . .] i feel weird about it you being so much younger than me and all*

shyshiagirl: *ur not old. dont feel weird*[30]

In the final episode, an assistant district attorney from Rockwall County (Texas), William Conradt, told his decoy that he decided not to come over. Perverted Justice pleaded with him to please make the effort: '*Are you gonna come or not? Well, when are you gonna com overrrrrr?*'[31] Conradt would have known that statute 33.021 in the Texas penal code makes it clear that an adult offends when he 'communicates in a sexually explicit manner with a minor', or someone under the age of 17.[32] And yet, over the course of two weeks, he developed a sexually explicit relationship with 'Luke', an 18-year-old Californian passing for a 13-year-old. The reality TV show was pulled after Conradt took his own life; police discovered his body while trying to serve him with a search warrant at his home, with the cameras rolling outside.

It didn't take long for critics to form a queue. Charlie Brooker, writing in *The Guardian*, ridiculed NBC's defence that the show encouraged parents to talk to their children about 'stranger danger'. Moreover, by paying Perverted Justice handsomely for their service (rumours have it that NBC paid the group a retainer of between $100,000 and $150,000),[33] NBC had created a potential conflict of interest. That they worked so closely with the police also meant a blurring of lines between private individuals and law enforcement such that an entrapment defence might actually stick in a court of law. Brooker then broke down the process of selecting 'child' actors by NBC, all of whom, for maximum impact, must look like a minor and be physically attractive or, as Brooker put it: 'hot' and US legal at age 18.

> Presumably someone at *To Catch a Predator* HQ sat down with a bunch of audition tapes and spooled through it, trying to find a sexy 18-year-old who could pass for 13. They'll have stared at girl after girl, umming and ahhing over their chest sizes, until they found just the right one. And like I say, she's hot. But if you fancy her, you're a paedophile.[34]

Brooker ends his critique thus:

> It's a pity robot technology isn't more advanced than it is, because the ultimate *To Catch a Predator* show could do away with the actress altogether. Instead, the men would be greeted by a convincing 17-year-old android, who'd

instantly start having sex with them. But oh! Just before they reached climax, a hatch would open in the top of her head, and a robotic version of Chris Hansen's face would emerge on a big bendy metal neck, barking accusations at them, and then the android's vagina would snap shut, trapping the pervert in position, and the robot body would transform into a steel cage from which they couldn't escape, and start delivering near-fatal electric shocks every five minutes to the delight of a self-righteous, audience, chanting Justice Prevails, Justice Prevails. Justice Prevails.[35]

Despite plenty of criticism, the reality series reverberated well beyond America's borders. In 2010, Channel 5 reporter Jason Farrell carried out a 'sting' on Simon Beard. In 2008, CSI Miami released *To Kill a Predator*, the seventeenth episode in season 6 of the TV series. In 2009, ITV screened *To Catch a Paedophile* while in 2010, German TV aired its own variety of the original NBC Dateline series, called *Internet Tatort*. In 2011, BBC2 released *The Paedophile Hunters* while in 2012, Canadian TV screened *To Troll a Predator*. By 2011, the archetype of the 'paedophile hunter' was already well known; ordinary folk have woken up to the idea that they could help catch and then expose those posing a threat to children.

One of the first to do so here in the UK was Keiron Parsons using the pseudonym of Stinson Hunter. He went on to star in the Channel 4 documentary *The Paedophile Hunter*. Like the original US series, this programme made for a riveting hour of television – it got a BAFTA award and plenty of approval – and led ordinary people to reconsider their vocation.[36] Within five years, a small handful of hunters grew to 191 teams known to the police that, between April 2019 and March 2020, notched up 1,310 confrontations with suspected paedophiles.[37] One undercover police officer described hunting as 'shooting fish in a barrel' to reflect the magnitude of the challenge facing society. Of these 191 groups, 57.6 per cent were involved in more than one incident, while one in five were involved in ten or more, and five were responsible for at least forty incidents each. It was one of these teams that I joined for four years (2018–22) and, for one of these years, it was responsible for more arrests than any other group.[38]

These figures suggest that a relatively small number of groups are responsible for most confrontations and that the majority don't survive beyond their first few confrontations with predators. In fact, the National Crime Agency estimates that 70 per cent of those who try their hand at paedophile hunting pick up sticks shortly after for reasons that are not entirely clear.[39] Anecdotal evidence suggests that talking to paedophiles online is more traumatising than many assume and, aside from the emotional toil, the late nights, busy weekends and long car journeys are an off-putting bar for the hardiest. Nor are many first-hand experiences of a sting as emotionally fulfilling as expected and, having done it once, some throw in the towel. Others may find that they and their peers aren't kindred spirits after all, leading them to set up shop with different companions under a new name.

After a pre-lockdown peak, the number of incidents dropped ever so slightly. There were 1,148 confrontations between hunters and predators between April 2020 and March 2021 involving one or more of 145 active groups, rising again post-pandemic to 1,410 incidents during April 2022 and March 2023 but spread across only 104 groups. On top of the hundred or so monthly arrests instigated by well-organised citizen activists, police take another 400 paedophiles into custody every month following their own investigations. The National Crime Agency thinks it highly likely that the true scale is far higher than suggested by the above data.[40]

The latest available data suggests that one in every seven stings takes place in London with the West Midlands, Yorkshire & the Humber and the East Midlands not far behind.[41] Nearly 41 per cent of all stings are 'meets', meaning that predators agreed to meet their 'child' in a public location, most often a train station, hotel, car park or fast-food outlet. The remaining 59 per cent are 'door knocks', where hunters will have found out where a predator lives or works and take their grievances to where it likely hurts most.[42] Most hunting groups operate in isolation, and when they do cooperate with others it is either because a suspect lives too far outside their typical geographical area (even though some hunters won't think twice of driving up to four hours one-way to confront a predator), or because they don't have the numbers needed to provide security on a particularly perilous estate, or because more than one team had been 'talking to' the same predator and in sharing intelligence they decide to also share the sting and credit.[43]

When, in August 2018, I threw my lot in with that of paedophile hunters I quickly found myself in the company of factory foremen, hospital porters and those working on building sites; a few were ex-military and several worked the doors of pubs and night-clubs; and though there was the odd barrister, solicitor, journalist, stockbroker and entrepreneur, white-collar workers seemed the exception. Government estimates subsequently confirmed my suspicions that those who take up hunting disproportionally represent the working classes.[44] So why do hunters not represent more segments of society seeing as abusers do?

When testing this observation with those close to – but not inside – the hunting community, responses vary. Some think the working classes tend to sort out any problems between themselves, much as the IRA was known to do.[45] This is, they say, preferable to relying on law enforcement to deal with social deviants. Others suggest that too few among the working classes have much reason to champion the police (about half of all hunters in the greater London area have a criminal record).[46] Yet others put it more crassly by saying that not having meaningful employment means that hunting fills an existential void or that a feeling of disenfranchisement from the political process means that hunting stands in for political participation. Or, say yet others, maybe hunters are simply more likely to have experienced abuse and thus have good reason to protect those unable to fend for themselves. I won't wager which of these answers are correct, I simply do not know, but nor would I be surprised if there wasn't a little bit of truth in each of these.

Distrust of law enforcement is rife within the hunting community, even if suspicions are more typically aimed at senior members – or the managerial elite – than at those policing the streets. But a lack of confidence in the powers-that-be has led to some interesting initiatives by citizens. One of these is a searchable online register of convicted offenders and those who allegedly pose a threat to children. Members of the public are warmly invited to send in names and details of those they suspect of harbouring an unhealthy interest in kids, with the predictable result that some use it to crucify those they can't stomach.[47] Others have improved on the above by way of a database of sex offenders that allows for anonymous submissions provided that they are backed by an official source, such as the police or news media.[48] Then there are those who are less interested in creating these public databases than leveraging existing ones. By relying on public sector employees with access to databases, for example, they

can access details on the whereabouts of suspected predators in prep-
aration for a 'door knock' at home or place of work.

Most teams make it a point never to ask the public for
financial support, and not because they don't have use for funding
(petrol costs alone can match a weekly household budget) but
because they are keen to avoid the impression that they are doing
this for improper motives. As always, there are exceptions. Some
raise funds by selling merchandise through their websites while
others ask their members for subscriptions.

While the police prefer hunters not to interfere with law
enforcement, they also know that child sexual abuse online isn't
a problem they alone can solve. Paedophile hunters have been
known to pick up predators that do not show up on the police
radar yet can be dangerous to children. Moreover, evidence offered
by hunters has previously helped convict paedophiles in courts of
law. This evidence always includes screenshots from exchanges
between a predator and child (often a decoy), where each screenshot includes the last lines of chat from the previous screenshot to
make sure to leave no gaps in the conversation. Oftentimes the
evidence includes images sent by the predator to the child, 'dick-
pics' mostly but also masturbation, adult porn and much, much
worse.

In 2019, the BBC asked forty-five police forces in England,
Wales, Northern Island and Jersey to tell them how many convictions relied on evidence supplied by paedophile hunters. Forty-two
forces responded. Their data showed that 403 people were prosecuted in 2018 for attempting to meet a child following online
sexual grooming; 252 of these cases involved evidence gathered
by hunting groups. Thirty-three forces supplied all that had been
requested under the Freedom of Information Act, revealing that the
number of cases involving hunter evidence had more than tripled in
the space of two years, rising from 57 in 2016 to 179 in 2018. The
proportion of cases involving this evidence had also grown, from
less than 25 per cent of cases in 2016 to more than 60 per cent of
cases in 2018.[49] Up to 80 per cent of suspected predators exposed
by hunters between April 2017 and August 2018 weren't known to
the police as posing a threat to children at all.[50] A subsequent
internal questionnaire completed by police forces in early 2023

suggests that they used evidence packs produced by hunters in police investigations in 90 per cent of cases.[51]

When police arrest a suspected predator, the legal basis for doing so is often Section 67 of the United Kingdom's Serious Crime Act of 2015, which made sexual communication with a child a criminal offence. In a recent ruling to extend four prison sentences, the UK Court of Appeal was explicit in ruling that 'sentencing should be set by reference to the harm that the defendant intended to cause the fictional child'.[52] This suggests that it makes no legal difference whether the child in question is real or an adult posing as a child, nor does it matter if the defendant believes he was communicating with someone over 16 as long as the 'child' in question repeatedly told him their 'pretend' age (typically between 11 and 15).[53]

The law applying to photographs says that one must be at least 18 to appear in a sexual image (even though the legal age of consent in the UK is 16). This means that predators who ask children for nude images or webcam sex quickly find themselves in difficult waters. Even drawings and AI-generated images that feature children in compromising situations are illegal to produce and also to view in the UK.[54,55] Those caught are required to sign the Sex Offenders Register at a local police station within three days of conviction or release from prison (if given a custodial sentence) or else risk facing yet another criminal charge.[56]

Of four different charges that could be levied against those holding sexual images of children, possession of 'first-generation' pictures is the worst by far as it implies the creation of a new image rather than the distribution of an existing one.[57] Of course, that no first-hand encounter between predator and child took place does not absolve the predator: sharing or viewing second-generation images is not a victimless crime of course, as viewing them means more demand for them.[58]

These realities mean that police find themselves in an unenviable position. While they say they welcome the involvement of citizens in fighting crime, they cannot publicly legitimatise hunting given the harm hunters cause, and nor is it easy for them to do so legally. Were police to proactively work with hunters, they would likely have to treat them along the same lines as undercover agents, meaning that hunters would be bound by similar restrictions on evidence gathering.[59] Currently, they accuse hunters repeatedly of acting on insufficiently robust evidence and of jeopardising ongoing investigations, of failing to safeguard suspects with learning difficulties who may prove difficult to prosecute (yet are involved in 25 per cent of all incidents[60]), and of not taking care to protect suspects and their families from reprisals by neighbours. There are known cases of hunters using physical force with suspects. In one instance, hunters dragged a suspect out of a corner shop where he had sought refuge, for which they were summarily arrested and charged, albeit acquitted in court. There are also plenty of instances where suspects and their families were harassed or abused by members of the public following a confrontation. If only their evidence were foolproof: in nine confrontations between April 2017 and September 2018, the suspect was considered unlikely to have offended at all, and in five of them, hunters even identified the wrong person altogether.[61] Some hunters have also been accused of using stings to extort money from suspects, and while blackmail is illegal, paedophile hunting isn't. If anything, it enjoys some support by courts: nearly every case against hunters so far has been decided in the hunters' favour. Thus, police are understandably reluctant to engage with them other than arresting predators for fear of being seen to sanction, or turn a blind eye to, harmful activities. And yet by distancing themselves from hunters, they are less able to contain the devastating consequences of hunters' actions for those suspected of abusing children but are yet to be convicted of any offence.

This book is intended to bring you up-close to the messy world of paedophile hunting. It hopes to give you a better idea of what motivates ordinary people to take it upon themselves to rid society of sexual deviants by whatever means necessary. It hasn't any scholarly pretension, even if it is based on rigorous research.

Also, ethnographers tend to worry a great deal about how their accounts will be received by the people who feature in them, and I'm no exception. The title of Carolyn Brettel's book *When They Read What We Write* captures this anxiety well. So, what I decided to do was ask hunters and police to respond to the book and let readers know where they thought I got the wrong end of the stick (and hopefully where I occasionally got it right too). They were happy to oblige. You will find their reflections at the very end.

3

It takes me a while to find space to park on a busy road into a northern English town. I haven't any idea how long a walk it is to our meeting place but am damn sure I do not wish to arrive early. I know they'll be watching me, and being watched means that I get self-conscious and being self-conscious makes me act unnatural and acting unnatural raises suspicion.

How long do I want to park for? my app wants to know. I best be generous, I think, just in case today's conversations take off and besides I haven't anywhere else to be. Yet I also want to have a believable excuse to take my leave should things get out of hand or if all of it ends up feeling like a waste of time. Using an app to park means that I can buy extra time at any point during the day, and the hunters will know this too, and so how will I dodge their questions if the parking is what I'll choose to rely on to flee the scene? Am I overthinking this?

One might assume that anxieties recede into the background with time and experience. But for me they never did, and not even after having been 'in the field' for much of the past fifteen years: with doctors and nurses at war, Cambridge Boat Race crews, adventurers on the river Amazon, peace activists on a walk to Aleppo. Of course, it may be that experience wises us up to how easily things can go wrong, and that's why. Or perhaps it is that I feel a peculiar unease around child abuse that I don't yet fully understand.

Seeing how hard hunters work at getting public opinion to weigh in on their side, I felt sure that any of them would happily have me tag along for a while. So I reached out to a few teams via Facebook but, to my surprise, without getting as much as an acknowledgement in return. As days, and then weeks, went by I worried that I might need to change course and opt for a more feasible research topic.

Then, late one morning, I received a note from someone who'd only just taken up hunting, and did so entirely on his own, to avenge a friend who'd been abused as a child. He was fine talking by phone, he said, and so we did later that day. He told me that his first sting had been coordinated with a group of hunters up north and, if I liked, he could give me their number. Their founder was a woman who knew the hunting community well and might help me find a footing. 'Just tell 'em I said that you should be talking to them,' he said, and when I did, was told that it might be best if we met face-to-face. If I were happy to make the trip up, she would make it worth my while by bringing along hunters from local teams. And it was this invitation that brought me here today.

I had timed things surprisingly well. As I enter the town square, I see a woman in her late thirties making a beeline for me. She looks no different from any of the shopping public except for a big smile. Hugging feels awkward at this early stage and so I give her my hand. She seems unsure how to respond and asks if I'm okay going to Spoon's for a chat?[1] 'Sure,' I say. As we head for the pub, we are joined by three men and a woman, one at a time, who appear as if out of nowhere. I imagine they kept well out of view in a busy farmers' market. One of the men wears a red hoodie with the name of his hunting team in white across his arms and back. Another wears blue, a third green. The woman is entirely in black and, unlike the men, wears a facemask featuring razor-sharp teeth. I do a double-take and daren't look at her again for fear of giving offence.

But first impressions deceive and before long, and after an order of drinks, we've warmed to each other. Would it be okay if I recorded our conversation, I ask and, when no one minds, I place my smartphone on the table. I tell them it's fine for them to switch off the voice recorder at any time should they wish to talk off the record and hand each of them an informed consent form to sign.

This raises no end of confusion: should they sign with their real name or the alias they use online or how they refer to each other within their teams? Seeing how reluctant they are to give their real names, aliases may have to do. Except of course that these tend to be generic, particularly when it comes to their 'alias last name' which usually signifies their role: 'Hunter' for hunters and 'Decoy' for decoys. If they sign using their aliases, will these 'contracts' still be 'binding'? And what if they don't want to give away *any* personal details?

And so what should have been a straightforward box-ticking exercise neutralised the vibe we'd spent a good amount of small talk nurturing. But we get there in the end. I tell them to be as creative as they like in signing off, assuming that so long as they'll be able to recognise their own aliases, we'll have satisfied the spirit of informed consent. I decide not to worry how to defend the mess if challenged by my university.

Around a small table, and furthest away from any natural daylight, the hunters talk with obvious resentment about what brought them to hunting in the first place. They tell me how distrusting they are of the police. The woman in the mask says how she was sexually abused by a senior police officer and how – here she uses colourful language – he ended up walking free. The one in a red hoodie was frequently beaten by his dad, who would also lock him up and starve him for days on end. The one in blue says that as many as eight out of ten hunters were abused as children. No source is cited but it isn't hard to believe, for even the police think that hunters represent a disproportionate number of survivors of abuse compared to the general population.

The one in green is sure that predators want to be caught, or some of them anyways, and even if they don't, 'when you show them the evidence you have on them, you can see their arseholes fall out'. 'And when you see that happening,' the one in red adds, 'it vindicates absolutely everything.' I am tempted to ask whether people might simply be surprised when suddenly faced with accusations of depravity regardless of whether these are true or not, and so that to see a target getting scared may not be the most robust indicator of guilt. But I let matters be. There's no point risking an argument this early in the fieldwork when everything still feels so delicate.

The masked woman meanwhile has moved the conversation back to the police, saying how they take far too long to turn up after they've been told that a predator's been caught and needs arresting.

'Six hours we had to wait once for them to finally show up,' she says. 'And the problem is that all the while we have to protect the predator from neighbours who are keen to have a go too.' The one in green says they had to protect a nonce from someone with a machete once, while the one in red tells us that he and his pals had to walk a predator to a police station three miles down the road because the police refused to come out in the snow. The one in blue says that he had to ask a predator to drive himself to the police station.

I find it hard not to feel sympathy when listening to their stories of neglect and abuse, and betrayal by those who should have been looking after them.

I call it a day after five hours of listening. Perhaps because we've begun to go round in circles. Or perhaps because they are heavy smokers and take to wandering in and out of our chat throughout the afternoon to smoke outside, which makes it difficult to sustain a meaningful conversation. And so, I figure I might as well call it a day and return to them what is left of theirs.

As I pack up my gear, the one in red asks me if I've heard of Oliver Braid from Wolf Pack Hunters, based in Scotland. Wolf Pack were early arrivals on the hunting scene, he says, and so maybe I should try to speak to them if I wanted to know more about the rougher side of hunting. He gives me a number and I call Oliver the next day.

4

Oliver and I are at a downtown Glasgow police station killing time. A few hours ago, we'd forced the arrest of a predator who spent weeks grooming a 14-year-old boy, not realising that this 14-year-old was Oliver pretending to be a child. The police say they want us to provide witness statements but seem happy to keep us waiting while they get their affairs in order. I decide that I may as well use this time to get to know Oliver. We spoke by phone but only met early this morning after he invited me to join him for my first-ever sting.

I activate the voice recorder on my smartphone. Here is what he says:

> Last time I was here, I came in a police car with this officer who was telling me off for the entire journey, saying that she was going to release our guy because she couldn't accept my evidence, even though he'd been talking to a 15-year-old, a 14-year-old, and a 12-year-old. I'd given her 700 pages of chat on this guy grooming three kids. I mean, Christ!
>
> Problem was that she had never dealt with a case like this and so I told her 'we've done seventy of these so we know how this goes', and still she wouldn't phone the CID [Criminal Investigations Department]. She was like 'CID won't come out for this' and that was the end of our conversation except that she kept me for another six hours until she finally got hold of a sergeant who told her exactly what I'd said six hours ago: that the guy we stung was a danger to children and she should go ahead and make the arrest.

She'd been saying that because there were two decoys on this guy and because the other decoy lived in another part of Scotland, it wasn't possible to make an arrest until this other decoy made a statement. And because this other decoy told police that she didn't want to travel three hours just to give a statement, and because police didn't want to send an officer out to her to take a statement, she said that police are now going to have to release the predator.

After I'd finally given my statement to CID, she told me that she was in a bad mood because she tried to get the night off work to go to a wedding and she wasn't able to and so she was here dealing with us instead, and so maybe that's why she was being so difficult.

He tells me about a recent sting by another hunting team, TRAP.

One time Stevie Trap caught this predator who turned up with a chocolate cake and a penis pump, and then when they got to him, he jumped on a bus to get away. And so one of the hunters gets on the bus too and tells the driver that he is police and that the guy who just jumped on board is a paedophile. Now obviously, you're not allowed to do either of those things, but it worked brilliantly cause the predator jumped off the bus and ran away but tripped, and then just kind of stayed on the ground sobbing.

I think he ended up in a mental hospital but can't be sure.

And then you sometimes you do someone whose chat hasn't been that bad, kind of like the one we did this morning, even if they still broke the law, and then you find out that they end up getting a massive conviction after police seize their devices and find really nasty stuff on them.

The police are still nowhere in sight and so I ask Oliver how he came to hunting. He tells me that he founded Wolf Pack with a mate of his, Gordon Buchan, out of necessity. He'd secured a small grant from an arts foundation to bring an English hunting team across the border into Scotland as part of a wider community project, but when the team pulled out, he felt he had no option but to start his own if he was to deliver on his promise. Gordon was an obvious choice as co-founder: he had been tortured as a child by his father before social services moved him into an indifferent care system. His inability to process his past led him to become hooked on drugs and he ended up running up a debt with a brutal group of gangsters who, in case he ever doubted their seriousness, knocked out several of his teeth.[1] One, and then more, prison terms followed before Gordon decided that enough was enough. Instead of continuing his destructive run, he was going to spend his time avenging himself on those who get their kicks out of molesting kids. Wolf Pack took no time to make a name for itself for being unusually aggressive, even as the hunting community found itself on the cusp of a move towards professionalisation. Led by teams such as COBRA, Silent Justice and Keeping Kids Safe (KKS), hunters began to wear 'uniforms' (hoodies with the team logo), to put in place 'after care' teams and, more generally, to refrain from intimidation and verbal abuse.[2]

Oliver tells me something else about himself too, which feels relevant to his interest in hunting. He'd been raised in a violent household, he says, which meant that he learned to find the sound of aggression strangely soothing. Hunting offers him the 'beauty of violence in its undiluted, rawest, from-the-gut form'. It is also why he likes listening to recordings of stings while doing stuff around the house – 'kind of like how people listen to music while working,' he says – finding comfort in the violence and humiliation. He also says that he's pretty sure his dad would have been picked up by hunters had he been alive today, given his interest in young women. I do not pursue the matter. He then tells me how he came to terms with his own sexuality, that what helped him was chatting online with grown men when he was only a 13-year-old, and he wasn't bothered by how sexual these chats became. He says that his parents' homophobia was far more traumatising for him than any of the stuff he'd found online, no matter how explicit.

At last, Oliver and I are called in to give our witness statements. We each follow a different officer into separate rooms. Mine wants me to talk him through the day from start to finish. And so I tell him how Oliver decoyed as a 14-year-old boy and was picked up online by a 30-something-year-old man interested in sex; how the man had told 'the boy' that he'd like for them to cuddle up naked under a blanket and see where that might lead; that he worked at a local trampolining centre and could get him free tickets. The predator then left complimentary tickets to the centre for the boy, tied with a rubber band, on the concrete step to his apartment building. There'd been a strong wind and so he must have only placed them there moments before we arrived as they'd have been blown away otherwise, I say. I then tell him that Oliver and his team saw this as a sign that the predator had hoped to meet the child, meaning he was now fair game, and confirm what he already knows: that the evidence pack itself is probably kind of on the slim side. What I don't tell him is how Oliver asked me before setting off whether I thought the evidence sufficient to warrant a confrontation, and how I didn't know seeing how inexperienced I was. Either way, Oliver was determined to get this predator off the streets.

There's something else I don't tell the officer: that Oliver had once been out on a date with our suspect a while back. But I tell him most of the rest.

Thirty minutes prior to the sting we met up with three other hunters in a supermarket carpark, agreed over smokes who would do what and when and, hoping to keep at a distance should things get violent, that's when I offered to call the police when given the nod. The atmosphere was one of excitement, part naughtiness, part 'fuck you', and partly the conviction of holding the moral upper hand. We split into two cars and set out.

It didn't take long to pull up at the predator's address and park out of sight around the corner of a tall Victorian block. We walked up several flights of stairs to the top floor, where Oliver knocked hard on a front door. The suspect's flatmate opened up and more or less told us straightaway that the guy we were looking for wasn't in and swore on his nan's life that he didn't know where he was. Oliver hadn't any time for excuses and addressed the predator directly through the half-opened door, telling him that he knew he was hiding inside, that they'd wait as long as it took and, in a colourful monologue over several minutes, sketched out a picture of the near future. Wishing to end the horror show once and for all, the flatmate put his shoulder to the door. No sooner had he done so than one of the other hunters began pushing hard from the other side, resulting in a toing and froing that stopped only once our persistence was rewarded: a voice from somewhere deep inside the apartment shouted for us to fuck off. On Oliver's nod, I made the call.

Police pulled up shortly after and ordered Oliver and me to make our way downstairs while they secured the suspect. Two officers took our details and ordered us to meet them at the station to give our statements. This isn't usually required in England, where police rely on a written witness statement, called an MG-11, instead; knowing that it'll be demanded, hunters typically include the MG-11 with copies of the sexual chat between predator and decoy. Three of our hunters had done a runner meanwhile because, by court order, none were permitted to be seen anywhere near each other, let alone for hunting. Were they found to be in violation of their bail conditions, they'd go straight to prison. This wouldn't have been an issue except that the police are now asking me to give them the names of all those at the scene. I tell him I don't know their names and it feels awkward, even disingenuous, to be deliberately vague in my responses to the police, but I figure that my loyalty is first and foremost to my fieldwork, and that if I'm able to pull off the fieldwork, the police would ultimately be the beneficiaries of it.

What is rather harder to conceal from Oliver is my telling the police that we met up in a supermarket parking lot; knowing it has CCTV, the police could easily find out the identities of those who joined the hunt. Thinking about how I may have compromised the operation leaves me feeling nauseated. It's as if I fell at the first hurdle by betraying the confidence placed in me by Oliver and his lot. All I want to do now is to go back to my hotel and shower off the day.

Will all future stings leave me feeling like this? Am I being too sensitive? I knew Wolf Pack took pride in their reputation for being mavericks and belligerents, and perhaps I should have expected nothing less. But it does make me wonder if it might be helpful to set boundaries on my involvement with these confrontations. I'd be fine phoning the police to make the arrest but otherwise much prefer not to be involved. However, and as has often been the case in my fieldwork, this is far easier said than done.

There's scarcely any love lost between Wolf Pack and the police. Wolf Pack are known (some would say admired) for their contempt of law enforcement. And they are effective in getting predators off Glasgow's streets: from October 2017 to March 2019, Wolf Pack secured the arrest of 80 suspects following stings, 25 of whom entered a guilty plea or received a guilty verdict in court. This of course means that 55 did not. Even if no further action was taken by the police these 55 men would forever be seen as compromised in the public eye for engaging sexually with what they assumed were minors online. The evidence may have been weak, or the suspect was found to suffer vulnerabilities or perhaps they were able to pay for exceptional legal defence, but the point is that once exposed, there really is no way back to life as it once was. Some members of the public don't mind the severity of it, thinking that predators deserve what's coming to them, and even if predators may never have posed a danger to real children, they shouldn't have been talking to them in the first place.

And yet occasionally Wolf Pack's methods are too extreme even for their own ilk. One former member told a journalist that he walked out angrily after a chaotic sting in August 2018, saying his fellow hunters were 'thugs looking for mob justice'.[3] The member in question, Marcin Kuciak, referred to a man stung for having talked to a 12-year-old girl and said how Wolf Pack were keen to expose him. Shouting and swearing and with hoods pulled over heads, they created such a racket that neighbours pleaded with the police to remove Wolf Pack from the scene. It wasn't the first, or only, time the police were called in to calm tempers. Weeks earlier, Wolf Pack gathered on a housing estate in the West Lothian town of Armadale to interview a registered sex offender. Having made little effort to hide what they were doing there, a mob quickly gathered and promptly set fire to a car. Wolf Pack had been concerned that the man was living with children of a similar age to the one they had impersonated online, and hence the spirited atmosphere.[4] Police arrested the suspect, if only for his own safety, and told the crowd to go home.

More arrests followed with accusations that Wolf Pack tried to abduct Stuart McInroy, a notorious online troll and, when the abduction failed, assaulted him at a bus station in Edinburgh instead. It seems McInroy had sent the team a string of vile messages in which he detailed all manner of things he'd done to children, and it had taken the team two years to track him down. But it was McInroy's alleged threat to rape Gordon's youngest son that pushed Wolf Pack over the edge. They would have none of it and replied to McInroy's threats with punches and a Glasgow kiss.[5]

'This guy on our team headbutted Stuart straight in the face,' Oliver said, 'and then did a runner before police showed up, and so even though he caused all the damage, it was everyone else who ended up getting pulled in front of the sheriff.' Did they tell on the guy who did the headbutting, I asked. 'Didn't matter if we did or didn't,' Oliver said. 'Police knew who he was but just couldn't find him. And so several of Wolf Pack spent two weeks in jail while this guy was growing his hair out and trying to change his face and avoiding people because he knew police were after him.'

McInroy was no stranger to the sheriff either, having been jailed for ten months in August 2014 after claiming he had tortured and killed a 27-year-old, and then taunted the missing man's family with graphic details. Sheriff Weir banned three of Wolf Pack from engaging in vigilante activities for two years, and it was my complicity in this ban's violation that had made for an awkward confession.

Instead of heading back to my hotel, I take up Oliver's invitation for drinks and a spliff at his flat. He smokes far too much of the stuff, he tells me, lights up and offers it to me. He says:

Just feels like I'm fighting an endless battle managing Wolf Pack. Every time I sort one thing out something else happens, like a never-ending drama. I work like 35 hours a week and I still turn out one chat log a month whereas there are people in our team who've been here for months and still never handed in a chat ever. All they do is create drama. Why should I work for seven hours a day and then decoy for three hours when no one else is doing anything?

Despite this being the case, he says he enjoys stings 'cause they are so naughty'. He tells me about one where the predator and his pal had come out of a house together, one with a belt wrapped around his fist and another carrying a knife. Undeterred, one of Wolf Pack's picked up a brick and had it not been for police pulling up to separate the warring parties, things might have ended up in court. The last time they got dragged before a judge one of the women spat at the bench and was promptly given two additional weeks of jail time.

What I hadn't realised was that Oliver's long been on the radar screen of Saz, one of COBRA's co-founders. She's admired his stings from afar and it was Oliver's approval of me that shifted the odds of access to a local team in my favour. He gives me her email address and tells me that COBRA could make for a nice team to tie up with long term 'Let them know I sent you,' he says, and so I do, only to find that Saz and her husband, Jay, know all about me too.

Jay tells me that he'd like to interview me via Zoom, as if this were just another job interview, and seems far more relaxed than I am when we connect a few nights after Glasgow. He doesn't disguise the fact that they've done their reconnaissance. That I'd spent time with military doctors and nurses in Afghanistan was a definite plus and, I suspect, the thing that gets me over the threshold. For if the military took me on board, then why not them?

What I can't tell Jay is something I've learned the hard way in a decade-and-a-half of fieldwork: this isn't likely to end well. It isn't for a lack of diligence on my part to be true to the evidence – and true to my own positioning within the community – let alone for a desire to write salaciously and do the dirty on easy targets. It is simply because writing the lives of others invariably means crossing a line into worlds that were expected to be kept private. As Nancy Scheper-Hughes discovered in writing up her fieldwork in rural Ireland:

> Like the people of Ballybran and Springdale, the islanders were most offended by the fact that the private had become public – that the ethnographer had foregrounded what the people studied wish to maintain in the background.[6]

She quotes the village schoolmaster:

> It's not your science I'm questioning, but this: don't we have a right to lead unexamined lives, the right not to be analysed? Don't we have a right to hold on to an image of ourselves as different to be sure, but as innocent and unblemished all the same?[7]

It may not have helped that she titled her book *Saints, Scholars and Schizophrenics*. The issue is at least partly this: who can we, as ethnographers, really speak for?

Sociologist and ethnographer Harel Shapira wrote about his own difficulties in getting accepted by citizen activists hunting down illegal immigrants along the Mexican–American border. An official letter by Columbia University to verify that he was a bona fide PhD student hoping to study these Minutemen was much less effective than his impromptu revelation of being Israeli and the realisation of one of the Minutemen that his Glock-17 was the very gun used by the Israeli Defense Forces. 'I figured if it's from Israel you know it's gonna be quality,' his contact told him in what Shapira describes as a bizarre, if propitious, turn of events.[8] The Arizona–Mexican border was their Gaza, he explained, only to make an already awkward comparison yet stranger. Such anecdotes go to show that what opens doors may not be what we thought was our trump card.

Nick McDonell, a former war reporter, wrote of a similar challenge:

> For more than a decade I'd reported and written about Iraqis and Afghans caught in the American wars. But recently I'd stopped, no longer thinking myself an appropriate person to tell their stories. I had been wrestling with the idea that I ought to pursue some kind of intrinsically useful work ... and leave people who suffered injustice to write their own stories. Because, rather than experiencing injustice, I had in many ways been its beneficiary ... Was I then a tourist – or worse, a kind of profiteer?[9]

And so I accept early on that I'll never be able to give voice to paedophile hunters, or not perfectly and nor fully, and so won't pretend otherwise. What I may be able to do is to tell you what I saw, was told and overheard others say, and to give you my best attempt at an explanation that, while not the only one, feels right to me and is supported by the evidence. I decide to be open about my own foibles, doubts and misgivings so that anyone reading this account might construct out of it something like a reasonably useful picture of hunting life.

Jay and I talk for a good hour. Why don't you meet me and Saz in a local pub, he suggests. I say Sure, and so we do the following evening. It is then that Jay offers to train me up as a hunter and, as if to hurry matters along, invites me to join them on a sting the very next day. They tell me to delete my Facebook account and to set up a new one under an alias. They also make me promise to never comment publicly on the activities of other hunting teams. I do as asked and resurface twenty-four hours later as 'Jack Lenz'.[10]

5

Saz and Jay invite me into a dimly lit conservatory at the back of a semi-detached somewhere in middle England. Jay, heavily tattooed in a t-shirt and jeans, sits on an office chair while Saz and I make do on a sofa covered with a patchwork blanket. Succulents and souvenirs from faraway places give the space a distinctly Bohemian feel, as do bedsheets suspended from the ceiling to shut out any daylight and keep the real world firmly in view on adjacent monitors. A borealis of greens and blues (the reflection of a saltwater aquarium) dances gently to my left. A parrot, two parakeets, three cats and four dogs seem excited by my arrival and, like their owners, are generous to a fault with affection. They're happy to let their moulting drift on the flow of our conversation.

This then – about 10 square metres with a sofa and dining table-turned-desk – is the nerve centre of one of Britain's most prolific paedophile hunting teams. It is here that Jay reviews chat logs between decoys and predators when deciding whether there is sufficient evidence to go out and 'light someone up'. He is as aware as Saz and everyone else of how stings destroy lives. Few of those whose unmasking is live streamed on Facebook will ever recover from the damage to their reputations, even if no charge or conviction is ever made. And so Jay needs to be convinced, he says, that the logs aren't the one-off consequence of a booze-filled night but evidence of persistent and systematic grooming. For all practical purposes this means that the logs (screenshots of chat between predators and decoy) show sustained sexual conversation after a predator has been told three times that he's talking to a child.[1] Not all teams are as careful as they are, Jay says, wanting me to understand that COBRA are one of the most professional outfits out there.

Having satisfied himself that the suspect is 'a wrong 'un', Jay sends out a call on Facebook Messenger to see who's available to join the hunt, prints out the chat logs, burns them onto a DVD (just in case), and stuffs the lot into his paedo-pack. From this point until the actual sting can take anywhere from a few hours (if the predator is posing an immediate risk to a real child) to a couple of days and, where feasible, Jay will try to schedule two or more of them on a single day to make best use of everyone's time. They've done as many as six in a single week.

I ask Jay how many of these he's done since founding the team in April 2018 with Saz and Lenny. He says he doesn't remember but it must be well over 150. COBRA have since grown from 3 to 45 members, including decoys, security and researchers. But turnover is high, particularly among decoys who are on the sharp end of sexual chat by predators. Yet without the critical role played by decoys – who sit through days, and often weeks, of sordid talk and all manner of sexual grooming – predators would be left to do as they wish on-and offline. It is decoys who eventually pass all evidence to hunters so they can execute a sting. If it wasn't for Facebook as a platform to showcase evidence of COBRA's success, Jay says, they'd be missing out on a major recruitment tool.

One of the dogs has made herself comfortable on the sofa next to me. The vibe is relaxed. Saz smokes Marlboros from a carton on the armrest while Jay rolls his own from tobacco plucked out of a tin box. His roll-ups are barely wider than the filter tips he uses to cut the toxins. Life's expensive and while both are holding down full-time jobs, I can't imagine they are all that well paid. Considering how much of their own money they spend on petrol alone, and refusing to take donations, I'm finding it hard to see how they make it all work financially. But they do.

Jay and Saz are enjoying the chance to reminisce about hunting, and though they never talk publicly about other teams online, they do very much talk about them when it's just among themselves.

JAY HUNTER
Do you remember watching that sting of the dwarf?

SAZ DECOY
Christ that was bad –

JAY HUNTER
They picked him up under one arm each and carried him across the road and then while they was filming him asked him if he could kick himself in the head –

SAZ DECOY
God that was awful –

JAY HUNTER
Must have kicked himself in the head twenty times –

SAZ DECOY
But I get why they do it. They want to humiliate them like they humiliated a child –

JAY HUNTER
Quite enjoyed watching that to be honest –

I'd love to leave hunting behind, Saz then says, but once you've seen the horrible abuse kids face you cannot walk away from it. Jay nods. When I ask them what needs to happen if they are to stop hunting, Saz says it'll be for hunting to be made illegal. It is the only way they can walk away from it all without feeling guilty. They pray for this to happen, they say, so they can stop this and move on with their lives.

I ask them about their first-ever hunt.

SAZ DECOY
I thought we was going to get beaten up –

JAY HUNTER
First time is always hard –

SAZ DECOY
We was looking for a bloke and I prayed all night long we wouldn't find him –

It is then that I remember how Saz took comfort in seeing a blue neon cross nailed to the front of a church in Stoke Newington as we drove to what was my first sting with COBRA. It was visible for perhaps a minute or so in slow traffic before being obscured by flats, and she looked at it for as long as it remained in view. She is deeply and unashamedly spiritual, even if not tied to any organised religion, and nor am I convinced that she enjoys the stings quite as much as Jay does. Maybe it is because for Jay the matter is personal: as a young boy he witnessed ongoing abuse within his family but wasn't old enough to stop it. Today, at a bulked-up 6'2" he takes no prisoners when it comes to keeping children safe.

Our first sting turned into an eight-hour wild goose chase. I was glad for it, though I daren't say so. I hadn't much enjoyed the one in Glasgow and wasn't crazily keen on the prospect of bearing witness to a long sequence of more of the same over several years. Perhaps it's the confrontation that irks me – the squaring off and imminence of violence. Maybe it is the humiliation on display, no matter how deserved it may feel at the time. It means that I am not nearly as sorry as Jay is about how that night unfolded.

JAY HUNTER
There've been so many since then though –

SAZ DECOY
Remember the one with a mind of a 13-year-old and we didn't know that when we went to the door?

JAY HUNTER
Unfortunately, they're the dangerous ones as well –

SAZ DECOY
Mental health are more dangerous cause they don't have the conscience –

JAY HUNTER
They will turn up and will have sex with children –

SAZ DECOY
And then I got told off by others for putting my hands on him and consoling him –

JAY HUNTER

Thing is that you know you are destroying people's lives, but then you've got the other part of it is they are destroying children's lives –

SAZ DECOY

We both cried afterwards, didn't we? I said I couldn't do it no more. I feel like we was dancing with the devil –

JAY HUNTER

I'm different from her. I like to look them in the eye. I like to see them arrested. I like to see the cuffs on them. I like to see them taken away and I like them to know that I have done that –

SAZ DECOY

Coz you're stronger, that's why –

JAY HUNTER

I don't even know how they can watch child abuse images, to be fair. Makes me feel sick beyond belief. I think a lot of it is that you can access it so easily. If you go on the dark web, it's the first thing that comes up –

SAZ DECOY

On the dark web you're going to go into cults and things –

JAY HUNTER

Why are you suddenly going to go into cults?

SAZ DECOY

Because that's where they're saying paedophilia is mostly done at the minute –

JAY HUNTER

No, it isn't –

SAZ DECOY

You've not been watching the internet? It's a whole new thing. You'll see –

6

Everything about the old man repulses me and no matter how I much I want him to hurt, an even bigger part of me wishes the interrogation to be over with. Most predators don't seem to know why they do what they do in any event, and tilling the soil only stinks up the airwaves. I feel a strong pull to go home and be with what makes me happy, all of which feel worlds away from the drama unfolding before me.

I've been 'hanging out' with COBRA for a good while now, as is to be expected, and in so many ways, today's sting is typical: a predator confronted with his crimes tries his luck at persuading us that he was only playing along in what he thought was a game between consenting adults, never hurt anyone, and genuinely believed there wasn't anything wrong with what he was doing online. It is as if predators like him just cannot see themselves as anything like the monsters that regularly make headline news: those who groom, drug and pass around girls like candy; teachers, doctors and clergy who abuse positions of trust; parents who subject their own children to abuse. How am I anything like these awful monsters, they will ask themselves.

The old man will get his comeuppance to be sure, though I can't imagine it being worse than for him to know that his wife and sons will soon also know. To know that his grandchildren will be asked by police if granddad ever said or did things to them that didn't feel right. To know of the abuse his family will receive from online trolls, and how they'll be gawked at by neighbours when going about their daily routines. To know that kids at school will want to be in on every detail and will ask and tease. The old man will likely be remanded and never be allowed to see them again unsupervised, and nor is his wife likely to welcome him back. Nothing will be as it once was.

He's been made to stand against a lacquer-dipped panel fence. Hoarse from a cold, the old man fields one question after another in front of an online audience of COBRA members. Because today's sting involves a real child rather than a decoy, and to protect the child's identity, Jay decided to live stream it only in a private chatroom. No sting is worth putting a child further at risk, he says.

Facing the man are four hunters. They've 'encaged' him in case he does a runner. Other than being old – I'm guessing somewhere in his seventies – he has no distinguishing features. Thistly eyebrows frame the top side of his face, a beany on his head. His chin rests on a zipped-up collar which makes it seem as if he's wearing a neck brace. His trousers are dark, maybe black, hard to tell in twilight. Like most predators, he looks so ordinary. There isn't the slightest hint of the danger this man poses to children.

JAY HUNTER
So why was you recording your granddaughter – ?

OLD MAN
To talk to other people –

JAY HUNTER
Have you got an attraction to young children – ?

OLD MAN
No, no, no. It's only a habit –

JAY HUNTER
So you *do* have an attraction to young children – ?

OLD MAN
Only to look at –

For predators, it is usually best by this point to fess up and not make life more difficult for those who spent hours studying the chat logs, all of which are contained in a backpack. It also holds a portable battery pack, roll-up tobacco and a disposable lighter, a woollen hat, dark sunglasses and defective mobile phones to act as decoys in case police decide to confiscate everyone's phone as evidence. It is one of the older tricks in the hunters' book. Even if streaming live to Facebook means that no recording is ever held on camera phones, police still occasionally ask hunters to hand them over, in which case a quick and discrete swap means police get given a useless one instead. Smartphones are expensive and forensics can take months before finally returning them to their rightful owners.

JAY HUNTER
Where are you accessing them videos from – ?

OLD MAN
A Russian account –

JAY HUNTER
And then on top of accessing them videos, you're also live streaming your *granddaughter* –

OLD MAN
No. I was streaming me. Pretending to be her –

JAY HUNTER
I know you was pretending to be her. One of the titles of the videos you put up with your granddaughter says, 'later on I'm going to finger myself and I'm going to lick my fingers after' –

OLD MAN
Sorry –

JAY HUNTER
Have you any idea how many phones your granddaughter will now be on where men are getting off over her – ?

OLD MAN
That's my fault –

JAY HUNTER
It absolutely is your fault. You pretending to be a young child that looks up to you as a fucking hero, and you are destroying that poor little girl –

OLD MAN
Yes –

JAY HUNTER
Do you know how hard it is to stand in front of you after seeing what you did to your granddaughter – ?

OLD MAN
I used my granddaughter's photos but never did nothing to her –

JAY HUNTER
You *exploited* your granddaughter. What was you thinking of live streaming her – ?

OLD MAN
I was only using her to talk to other people –

JAY HUNTER
Those pictures on your phone, they are of your granddaughter aren't they – ?

OLD MAN
No they're not. I swear on anybody's lives –

JAY HUNTER
So, who is it then in the pictures – ?

OLD MAN
Don't know. Just pictures from the internet –

JAY HUNTER
So you like to watch children being raped – ?

OLD MAN
None of them are being raped –

JAY HUNTER
So they gave their consent, did they, when they're eleven, twelve years old –?

OLD MAN
I didn't film any of it –

JAY HUNTER
But you're watching them films and so you are participating and that's the reason these young children are raped to start off with. And so now what's the difference between that 11-year-old child and your granddaughter? That child is someone else's granddaughter –

OLD MAN
I've never touched any girl or anything like that –

JAY HUNTER
But you're happy for somebody else too –

OLD MAN
Am I gonna be arrested – ?

JAY HUNTER
You most certainly are. Police are gonna take all your electronical devices; they're gonna take everything that connects to the internet out of your property; they're gonna take that away and forensically download it to see just how many child abuse images and videos you either making or distributing –

OLD MAN
Fair enough –

JAY HUNTER
But it's not really fair, is it? Whose son has the child that you are doing this to – ?

OLD MAN
My youngest. Her mother's dead –

JAY HUNTER
Okay. So this poor little girl hasn't got a mom and so she comes around to nan and grandad's for support, and that is how you repay her –

OLD MAN
Sorry –

JAY HUNTER
How do you think your son's gonna feel when he finds out –?

OLD MAN
He's gonna think his dad is a bastard –

JAY HUNTER
Do you know what I would do to my dad if I found out – ?

The police will shortly be arriving on the scene, at which point the filming will stop. The police aren't keen on live streaming.

But despite heavy criticism from police and media, hunters persist with broadcasting their confrontation with suspected paedophiles, and what I'm keen to find out is why. They tell me it allows them to engage directly with online supporters and derive something like a democratic mandate for what they do. Any criticism of their methods expressed by any member of the public is swiftly and harshly dealt with, typically by suggesting that critics must be in on it.

So resistant is this online community to criticism, and so effective in policing itself, that it is virtually immune to any attempt by police to mitigate the harm of live streaming. Within law enforcement more broadly, there are plenty who suspect that hunting is seen as an effective means of lifting one's sense of self-importance or self-worth.[1] But beyond such suspicions, many admit to having no real insight into hunters' motivations (and refer to this as an 'intelligence gap') and acknowledge the need for a far more sophisticated understanding.

JAY HUNTER
Do you know that every single day people like us go out to protect children? We don't get a penny apart from a heart ache and tears for what we see. But every single day we drag ourselves back up and do it again to safeguard children from beasts like you –

OLD MAN
Sorry –

JAY HUNTER
And now your granddaughter needs safeguarding. What are you gonna do if she's walking home from school and she disappears because someone's infatuated with her because

of the videos you put out? When she's found in a ditch somewhere, how are you gonna explain that to your son – ?

OLD MAN
My sons will never talk to me again –

JAY HUNTER
How is that an answer to the question I just said to you –

OLD MAN
I will not explain it to him because he will he ever speak to me again –

JAY HUNTER
Oh, he's gonna have something to say unless he's in on it. Apple don't usually fall far from the tree does it – ?

OLD MAN
No, that's not right. He doesn't know –

JAY HUNTER
So then why is he letting her spend so much time with you?

OLD MAN
She only comes during the day –

JAY HUNTER
So how are you able to film your granddaughter's under-wear if she doesn't sleep over at your house? Because in your videos, yeah, you're sexually aroused by your granddaugh-ter's underwear and that's about as messed up as it comes –

OLD MAN
My son brings their laundry to our house every week –

JAY HUNTER
I bet you're straight in there like a lucky dip –

OLD MAN
That's not how it is –

JAY HUNTER
I mean it's so badly wrong, isn't it? Your wife's going to know. And your work mates. What d'you do for work – ?

OLD MAN
I'm retired. But I drive children to school –

JAY HUNTER
You do what?

OLD MAN
I drive children. Disabled. I drive them to school –

JAY HUNTER
Jesus Christ –

OLD MAN
It isn't how you think it is –

JAY HUNTER
It's *exactly* how I think it is. You must be like a kid in a fucking sweetshop, aren't you, picking up those children –

OLD MAN
Please can you phone the police again – ?

JAY HUNTER
So, after you've had your sexual gratification yeah, what d'you do? You roll over and go to sleep –

OLD MAN
No –

JAY HUNTER
Do you never once think about what you done – ?

OLD MAN
I think about what I done every time I done it –

JAY HUNTER
So why keep doing it – ?

OLD MAN
Don't know. I tell myself no more every day –[2]

With the arrival of the police, the sting's a wrap. Thankfully, the police don't ask for our phones (I haven't a spare one on me, unlike Jay), and it is one reason why hunters prefer to broadcast live. When asked, they say that live streaming is necessary because most predators will be out on bail shortly after arrest and the communities in which they live – their neighbours and their friends – have a right to know. Moreover, live streaming allows for other teams to identify predators they have also been talking to online (because online abusers often talk to more than one 'child' at the same time), and so can add their evidence to that already available.

Many also claim that live streaming puts online abusers on notice by showing them what will happen if they continue the abuse. I've heard hunters say that it offers proof of guilt when predators confess to their perversions on camera, and that it protects hunters against accusations of manhandling the suspect. Some even think that the police turn up more rapidly when they know a sting is being live streamed and that, besides, live streaming isn't punishment.

Yet these arguments are relatively easily undermined when considering that one could use a GoPro to do the recording (meaning that police wouldn't need anything other than take a relatively inexpensive memory card). Moreover, it is unlikely that neighbours of predators will be watching stings online, and even if they did, they may well seek retribution before a conviction in court has been secured. Also, any confession is unlikely to be admissible if obtained on film under duress, and any predators watching stings online are more likely to go underground than to stop the abuse. As for preventing accusations of abuse themselves, hunters could just as easily train their camera on the suspect's body instead and thus avoid showing his face or agree to release the footage only after a conviction had been secured in a court of law.

And insofar as broadcasting confrontations isn't punishment, those on the receiving end of it are quite likely to experience it as a form of punishment more severe, and more permanent, than any physical harm.

The most plausible reason given for live streaming, then, is that it provides hunters with a public mandate. Viewing figures, after all, can tally upwards of half a million views in a matter of days and teams like COBRA are keenly tuned into how many watch their handywork online. As one of the team wrote in a team chat: 'The 2 we did this weekend have some great exposure ¼ million and 200 thousand.' It is far easier to attract 'eyeballs' to 'live' or 'almost live' stings than to pre-recorded ones, as Jay and others readily admit. This is also one reason why the police suspect hunters of being more interested in pursuing Facebook likes than in getting predators convicted.[3]

Aside from 'eyeballs' offering hunters a democratic mandate, how else might we explain the persistence of live streaming? Might we be able to frame this phenomenon along narrative lines? After all, if one is prepared to consider that hunters may be acting out an old and deeply familiar narrative,[4] it is possible to see live streaming as integral to it. For example, a hunter might conceivably think of himself as the archetypical superhero who sets out to rescue a damsel in distress from an evil monster and, in doing so, saves his whole community. This would make hunters society's last line of defence in that those formally charged with protecting it have failed to do so or shown themselves incapable or unwilling. Having restored the moral order, the superhero would recede once more into obscurity.

The characters in this narrative feed off each other: the more impotent the police or parents or other institutions are perceived to be, the more vulnerable the child, the more beastly the monster, the more heroic the hunter. This would explain why hunters refer to sexual predators as 'monsters' and 'beasts' that prey on 'the innocent' and why they constantly remind each other to 'keep safe' prior to any and every sting even as hunters heavily outnumber predators in most cases. Also, the superhero's motivations are framed to offer a stark contrast to those of the monster.[5] And of course this monster poses a threat not just to a 'damsel' – which, like the child, invokes innocence, purity and vulnerability – but to a whole way of life, meaning that our superhero gets drawn into a struggle between good and evil 'to save all those who are suffering in the monster's shadow; to free the community or the kingdom the monster is threatening'.[6]

If the flatness of such narratives and their characters feels familiar it is because they resemble fairy tales, where characters are often clearly drawn, and where details, unless absolutely critical, are eliminated.[7] Stories cast in this mould are popular precisely because they reflect universal human concerns.[8] They offer hunters a narrative logic that helps render their activities as meaningfully related and pointed to a single, noble objective. And they offer an alternative explanation for hunters' persistence with live-streaming confrontations: they are the apotheosis of the hunter's quest. The sting then is the final battle between good and evil that tests the character of a hunter and must be played out before a live audience.

Any subsequent convictions in court are, for some teams, neither here nor there and thus what police assume is a means to an end, for hunters as heroes, is an end itself.

Even if hunters are never explicit about enacting this narrative, the evidence suggests that they act as if they are. To set their actions to a dramatic score offers a logic and justification for everything they do. The vulnerability of this narrative to complication or subversion explains why hunters are always on the defensive, for example by reminding each other at every sting to be careful. Of how dangerous and vile predators are, as if predators weren't outnumbered many to one. Of how they cannot walk out of the hunting life because no one else will step up to take their place. Of how the end game of keeping children safe justifies all means. For to ride out to protect the innocent effectively gives hunters a 'get out of jail free' card. And so in reinforcing the flatness of the characters that populate their existential narrative, they have produced an impregnable lifeworld in which zealous conviction, trauma and angst amplify each other.

It is of course easier to do what is difficult when satisfied that one is on the right side of the moral argument. 'If you are a paedophile, you have no right to privacy,' one online supporter wrote with another adding that 'if someone wishes to harm a child, they do not deserve human rights'.[9] Studies on public perceptions are unambiguous about strong feelings of anger and disgust towards sex offenders, particularly towards those targeting children, and the public remain doubtful that (more humane) treatments are ever effective. In fact, scepticism about paedophiles able to change their ways is 'probably the most deeply entrenched belief about sex offenders'.[10] That being the case, there are still plenty of people seeking help: in 2019, nearly 95,000 people from the UK contacted *Stop It Now*, a confidential helpline operated by the Lucy Faithfull Foundation designed to help those worried about having sexual thoughts and feelings about children;[11] there was a 119 per cent increase between 2018 and 2019 in the numbers of people asking the charity for help.[12]

But not everyone is supportive. There are people who worry that by live streaming stings suspected predators are not given the presumption of innocence that is their legal right. As someone said online: 'We live in a society whereby people are deemed innocent until proven guilty. Naming and shaming these people without a fair trial in court runs the risk of exposing an innocent person in error, having potentially horrific consequences.' Someone else said that hunting was 'mob justice' and another that 'people recording the video could have made this up and been themselves paedophiles too'.[13] Believing that the police are unable to tackle the challenge – something police have themselves acknowledged – others said that they simply no longer trusted the police to deliver justice and that 'police don't have the manpower and our kids are more at risk than ever with the internet and the hundreds of apps available'. Some suggested that police should work with paedophile hunting groups.[14] The National Society for the Prevention of Cruelty to Children (NSPCC) agreed. 'We need to know how forces and paedophile hunters can work together without jeopardising cases or potentially putting children in danger.'[15] These responses are typical of strong views held on both sides of the argument, and as such they echo a sentiment expressed by many.

Anxious about his immediate future, the argument will likely feel academic to the old man. His worry will be on how to get himself out of the hole he's dug and wondering if it may be best to pick up sticks and do himself in. Whether this troubles anyone, or whether I care, is altogether another matter.

7

In *Conversations with a Pedophile*, therapist Amy Zabin recounts a decade of weekly sessions and written correspondence with a notorious offender. Alan was arrested and convicted after confessing to sexually abusing over 1,000 boys between the ages of 7 and 13. Amy talks of how she was abused by her own father and paternal grandfather and how it was the need to understand her own abuse that led her to interview Alan.

Conversations feels a bit like a game of tag as Amy and Alan take turns offering a coming-of-age account of, in Amy's case, the abused and, in Alan's, the one doing the abusing. Alan tells us that he knew from an early age that he had an attraction to prepubescent boys, and that he became sexually active as early as 7 or 8 years old. His first experience of inflicting abuse involved a younger boy from his neighbourhood a year or two later. But even as he began masturbating at an unusually young age and had a strong attraction to other boys – and even as his abuse of others was distinctly sexual – the point of it never was. His abuse of others was, he says, about control.

> Many of my fantasies were built around the initial setup of placing a victim in a position where he was totally helpless. And these new feelings of increased power and control added a thrill that I had never experienced before and one for which I developed an insatiable appetite.[1]

And again:

> Anyone who looked at my life might easily believe that all the insanity was nothing more than a pathetic individual's attempts to find some type of perverted sexual gratification. But if you begin to carefully examine the process, to dissect the method by which I went about entrapping my young victims, and the pattern of my actions once I had manipulated a child to the point where he offered little or no resistance to my demands, a very different picture emerges. I am convinced that while there are many factors at work in my choosing to act out, the driving force, the element that triggered and spurred on others, was my insatiable obsession to feel that I had control.[2]

When his victims became too compliant or when sex felt too consensual, Alan lost interest and moved on to another victim or would escalate to a more extreme fantasy with the same victim. His approach was formulaic: he chose children well known to him, those whose parents he had befriended or those he babysat or mentored as a scout leader. They were never strangers. Having spent a great deal of time getting to know the family and child, he would groom the child into engaging in a sexual act by, for example, asking the child to take off his shirt or trousers and allowing Alan to take pictures. His biggest fear at that point, he said, was that the child might tell his parents of the abuse and so Alan's preoccupation became damage limitation. 'Under no circumstances was I going to take the child home until I had the opportunity to do everything in my power to control the situation.'[3] He reassured the victim by suggesting he'd made a 'once-in-a-lifetime' mistake, that he'd had too much to drink, and that something like it would never happen again, with the predictable result that the child would assure him in turn that all was okay, and that they were willing to forgive the error of judgement. Once a child felt sorry for him, Alan would play to their ego and greed by rewarding their friendship with gifts and flattery before confiding that he'd been in a similar situation before, with another boy, who had also proved to be a true friend by showing discretion. Invariably, the child wanted Alan to say more about this other boy and Alan would talk about a cousin of his who he'd done similar things to and who'd always been happy to forgive him for his errors knowing that Alan would make it up to him with special favours, and that this physical relationship continued but only at the request of his cousin, and only if he allowed Alan to do something for him in return. This cousin didn't exist except in Alan's imagination.

Alan and Amy's accounts are insightful in that they reveal a far greater threat to children, and one that is easily obscured by focusing on online predators alone. An estimated 75 to 95 per cent of offenders are known, and may even be related, to victims of abuse.[4] There are similarities between the grooming practices of Alan and those of online predators, the most striking of which is that the typical child molester is, well, 'typical'. He looks no different from any other member of the community, meaning that paedophiles hide in plain sight.[5] That seasoned hunters like Jay and Saz say that 'predators have this look about them' and that they can pick them out in public on any day may well be more telling of their own paranoia – the scar tissue of repeated confrontations with child abusers – than of paedophiles themselves.

There are also those who believe predators are disproportionately 'foreigners' and, even when born in Britain, of 'foreign' origin. Part of this misconception is fuelled by media reports of cruel and systematic abuse over many years by grooming gangs in Rochdale, Oxford, Huddersfield and Rotherham; gangs that were mostly made up of Asian men. But when considering arrest data, it quickly becomes obvious that most of those stung are British and white. And they are typically under the age of 30.[6] Those operating alone tend to be older than those operating in grooming gangs, and include all sorts: those of ostensibly stable, middle-class backgrounds as well as more chaotic lifestyles; those who are married and others who live alone; some already known to the police but then often only for minor priors.[7] When it comes to 'contact offences', where predators have set out to meet a real child, 'only' one-third involve men of a racial minority. For 'online offences', an estimated nine out of ten predators are white.[8,9] As predators tend to prefer victims of the same race, it is not entirely surprising then that by far the majority of children depicted in pornography are also white.[10]

Online sex offenders also tend to be younger than predators like Alan, better educated and more intelligent by ten IQ points.[11,12] Even so, nearly a quarter are subsequently diagnosed with vulnerabilities; typically, a neurodivergent condition (e.g., ADHD, autism spectrum condition or an intelligence deficit) or a mental health disorder.[13] Even if predators with vulnerabilities are not necessarily less dangerous to children, they do often prove more difficult to prosecute, and this is why police accuse hunters of wasting resources that could have been used instead to target more dangerous and better-organised offenders.

Nor is it true that all online predators subsequently turn to offending offline. Some predators develop an interest in child pornography out of curiosity but without a specific sexual interest in children, while others do have a sexual interest in children but won't move onto abusing them offline, even if their online antics make them complicit in fuelling the market for child sexual abuse and exploitation.[14] Yet others are involved purely for financial gain, hoping to make it rich at the expense of children. No matter their intentions, for the hunting public they are all fair game.

8

Hunters play a significant role in picking up predators not known to the police – some dangerous enough to be kept on remand and put behind bars – and contribute evidence that helps convict those who are known to the police in a court of law. Knowing this helps put the challenges facing law enforcement into perspective. The police do not currently have sufficient resources to tackle the problem of online child sex abuse on their own and without help from ordinary people, and yet they cannot be seen to condone any form of vigilantism. Like the Minutemen in Harel Shapira's *Waiting for José* – who claim they are the 'eyes and ears of the Border Patrol[1] – hunters are clear that they do not wish to usurp or replace the law and only help the police enforce existing legislation.

But knowing how helpful hunters can be, and yet how horrid the consequence for those falsely accused or families of the accused, police on the beat are often unsure how to best respond to stings except to make the arrest. This is why the National Police Chiefs' Council drafted a *Statement of Strategic Position* designed to help police speak and act with one voice. In it they acknowledge that tackling child sexual abuse is a high priority and that more needs to be done to build public confidence that the police are actively working to address it. They reiterate that they welcome active support from the public in identifying where children are at risk of being abused but make it clear that they find paedophile hunters unhelpful. Here is what it says:

> We do not endorse these groups and will not work with them. Unlike our officers, these groups don't offer any protection to victims, their evidence is often poor, and some do it as cover for extortion and blackmail. There are legitimate ways for the public to support the police and share information. Protecting children is a policing priority: every month we arrest more than 400 people for child sexual abuse and protect more than 500 children from harm.

For all practical purposes, this instruction tells police not to proactively engage with hunters but only to make an arrest when called upon as well as to investigate and safeguard the individuals involved. The problem, as the police see it, is at least twofold. First, the police think hunters are insufficiently targeted, meaning that hunters don't discriminate but will sting anyone who has been found to engage sexually with children. In contrast, they must prioritise the highest-level threats for the simple reason that total threat exceeds capacity. Because police must respond when called in to assist in a sting, it risks diverting resources away from higher-priority targets.[2] This might mean that a warrant against a predator who poses a high risk to real children will have to wait until police have 'processed' someone who sent sexual chat to a decoy but may not have physical access to children, nor ever wish to act on their fantasies.

Second, building prosecution cases from an unregulated practice is less efficient than following police procedure; hunters aren't always careful when it comes to issues of disclosure and fairness. Third, police are aware that less scrupulous hunters have occasionally used the threat of exposure to blackmail suspects into handing over money (a low-risk crime in that few victims will ever go to the police). To discern whether hunting is used to mask criminal acts through vetting takes effort, further diverting what are already scarce resources. Fourth, police believe that paedophile hunters don't always take sufficient care to safeguard suspects and their families from reprisals by locals living in their community and from self-harm and, moreover, target predators regardless of 'mitigating' circumstances (such as neurodivergence or learning difficulties). While teams like

Jay and Saz's are mindful not to live stream suspects who show obvious cognitive impairments, many are not. Fifth, unless hunters are careful, there is a risk that important evidence gets lost or missed after challenging a suspect and, sixth, that hunters and decoys risk entrapping vulnerable adults who would not otherwise have engaged in inappropriate behaviour, for example, in portraying themselves as more liberal sexually in chats than children typically do.[3]

But it is not just law enforcement that polices hunters. As a matter of fact, hunters do a decent job at policing each other. The result of this is a deeply judgmental, hostile and spiteful online community. This isn't to say by any means that all hunters are unpleasant – I've enjoyed meeting many of them and found them to be friendly – but that the search for purity in a morally complex world is more likely than not to result in polarisation along strongly expressed opinions and identities. Here's one of many examples of what I have in mind: a suspected predator got stung not once but twice, prompting condemnation from some in the hunting community.

LAURA DECOY
I don't understand this. This guy has already been charged and is in court on Monday, so why is this bloke going to his home to expose him? I hope all predators die a slow and painful death but this just doesn't sit right with me –

STU HUNTER
This must be a new thing these idiots just started doing intimidating him into pleading guilty at court –

HANNAH DECOY
This Paedo hunting team stung the guy and after exposing him, they exposed him again. Then after that, they exposed him again. But '3' times wasn't enough, so they exposed him a '4th' time. So on that note. Don't find it 'so' surprising. As for certain Paedo hunting teams, '1' exposure is 'never' enough. They have to do it over and over –

LAURA DECOY
But why? It doesn't make any sense!

STU HUNTER
It's called intimidation they are absolute idiots –

MAGGOT DECOY

Surely it will go in the favour of the predator as it will come across that he has been intimidated and therefore will not have a fair trial –

LAURA DECOY

That's what I think too Maggot, such a stupid, senseless thing to do and all he has achieved it to probably hlp the predator get a lesser sentence!

BLISS HUNTER

This video should be reported to the police, this scumbag is actually threatening this man into pleading guilty, we cant see this Hunters face, but he is clearly threatening & patronising this man into pleading guilty –

STU HUNTER

They have probably just messed the case up now by going to his home and intimidating him into pleading guilty at court. Absolute idiots they have no consideration for his sick elderly father who also resides at the address –

BOBBY HUNTER

WTF have I just watched? This man could've been handed a custodial sentence, like the team member said 'you belong in prison' well if his solicitor is any good then that will most definitely NOT be the case now. Absolute idiots!

EVA DECOY

Derbyshire Chief Police Commander has already asked these vigilantes to STOP, he states that they are wrecking police child exploitation investigations already ongoing –

STU HUNTER

Derbyshire police weren't wrong when they said these teams tend to catch the most vaunrable in society. This man is obviously a vaunrable adult he's about as dangerous as a toddler –

Feeling a little frazzled for the sordid theatre that is my world, I decide to accept an invitation from colleagues to meet for beers at The Mill, a pretty free house along the river Cam and across from Laundress

Green in Cambridge. From inside, I can see Darwin College's Newnham Grange, The Old Granary and Small Island, all at one time the playground of Charles Darwin's second son, George. The pub itself has a wooden bar top with eight handpumps – seven for locally brewed ales, one for cider – to help transfer ale from cask to glass. And it has a vintage radiogram that plays vinyl. By the time I walk in, my colleagues have already been drinking steadily for some time.

They ask about my fieldwork and so I tell them. One says that I must read Eric Hobsbawm's *Bandits* and so I do. And it's true that Hobsbawm's description of 'social bandits' feels familiar, and particular in relation to law enforcement and their online public:

> The point about social bandits is that they are peasant outlaws whom the lord and state regard as criminals, but who remain within peasant society, and are considered by their people as heroes, as champions, avengers, fighters for justice, perhaps even leaders of liberation, and in any case as men to be admired, helped and supported.[4]
>
> ... Insofar as bandits have a 'programme', it is the defence or restoration of the traditional order of things 'as it should be' ... They right wrongs, they correct and avenge cases of injustice, and in doing so apply a more general criterion of just and fair relations between men in general, and especially between ... the strong and the weak.[5] ... Whatever the actual practice, there is no doubt that the bandit is considered an agent of justice, indeed a restorer of morality, and often considers himself as such.[6]

Hobsbawm quotes Ivan Olbracht in support, for much the same reason I do:

> Man has an insatiable longing for justice. In his soul he rebels against a social order which denies it to him, and whatever the world he lives in, he accuses either that social order or the entire material universe of injustice. Man is filled with a strange, stubborn urge to remember, to think things out and to change things; and in addition he carries within himself the wish to have what he cannot have – if only in the form of a fairy tale. That is perhaps the basis for the heroic sagas of all ages, all religions, all peoples and all classes.

Why do we not see more social banditry in everyday life? As Gavin Weston asks,[7] 'Robin Hood mythologized social banditry with a rose-tinted hue and Disney immortalized with its 1973 feature-length animated film, and so what's not to like?' Ever the typical academic, Weston answers his own question: Robin Hood is the exception to the rule – or at least our caricaturing of him is – seeing how bandits were often more self-serving than that. Dick Turpin serves as a useful example in that he robbed from the rich but without then also redistributing his newly acquired wealth to the poor. Besides, historically they were also more ambiguous than the stereotype and neither valiant nor helpful to the rural poor.[8,9] I find this complexification of the character of social bandits helpful because it feels true. Hunters, as social bandits, are hardly saints. They are driven to do what they do by multiple motives – some of which they may not be fully aware of (and much the same way we are often not fully cognisant of how complexly intertwined our own motives often are) – including 'being society's last line of defence', 'restoring morality in social life', 'avenging their own childhood abuse' and, perhaps for some, 'glory hunting' (a pejorative term used within the hunting community to criticise teams who appear to do what they do for no other reason than to attract attention).

There is little doubt, for example, that like Hobsbawm's bandits, hunters see themselves as a last line of defence in a world where trust in politicians, the judiciary and policing is lower today than at almost any time in recent memory. Like social banditry, paedophile hunters see their mission as primarily one of administering social justice. They tinker with the social system (they are not revolutionaries), and protect, rather than subvert, human rights. Predators will likely disagree on that last point in thinking their rights to dignity and privacy greatly compromised through public exposure. It is interesting in this respect that no UK court has yet upheld any claim by any predator of their human rights (including that to privacy) having been infringed. Unlike social bandits, hunters seek retribution rather than redistribution,[10] fuelled by stories of injustice. In Britain, the Metropolitan Police in particular have been heavily criticised for being institutionally racist, sexist and homophobic in a damning report by Baroness Louise Casey following the murder of Sarah Everard by serving police officer Wayne Couzens; the failure to act on intelligence in arresting Stephen Port earlier and so prevent one or more of his four murders in East London; two serving officers having been found to have shared images of two murdered sisters on social media, referring to the sisters as 'dead birds'; a 15-year-old having been unnecessarily strip-searched by four male officers at her school; the arrest of serving police officer David Carrick who was found guilty of 49 counts of sexual abuse, including 24 of rape, against twelve women.[11] Casey's report left 150 Met police officers facing investigations of sexual misconduct or racism. Adding this to a tally of other examples of police misconduct nationwide, it isn't much of a stretch to imagine citizens taking over duties ordinarily carried out by police, under the 'if they won't, we bloody well will' rhetoric.

Along these lines it is interesting, if not surprising, that hunters regularly reassure each other that predators are dangerous, not only to children, and also guilty as charged. Prior to stings, the supposed danger they have to overcome shows up in members reminding each other online to 'stay safe', even if predators are typically outnumbered and more vulnerable than hunters. After stings, hunters will typically talk about how dangerous the predator was. They say how 'shifty he looked' or how 'his family acted suspiciously' and how reassuring it is that today's sting means there's 'another one off the streets'. It may have been a tough gig, but they did right, and that's the point. This ritual is played out on a larger scale online, within the wider hunting community, through posting daily reminders of the 'imminent danger' faced by children, and by publishing updates on prior targets who were subsequently convicted in court.

Likewise, beliefs about the incompetence of the police and judiciary are affirmed through regular reminders on Facebook and in team chats that 'the police should be grateful we are doing their job for them'. The urgency of their work is highlighted in discussions of instances where police were slow to follow up or where the suspect was either acquitted or received a sentence that hunters deem much too lenient. When confronted with such disappointing outcomes – as when a suspected predator is released without any charge at all – hunters take it as further evidence of police incompetence.

Today's discussion online is a case in point: it involves a predator in Southend-on-Sea who was stung after having spent weeks grooming what he thought was a 13-year-old girl. He sent her vivid descriptions – and if that wasn't enough also photographs – of what he was doing while thinking of her. Apparently, Essex police refused to look at the evidence, telling the hunting team that they'd take over the investigation and do it 'the slow way'. It seems that the delay allowed the predator to go underground. Online reactions to the police's handling of the case were ferocious, if entirely predictable:

DEBBIE DECOY
Our fucked up system for ya –

GARY HUNTER
If I saw him I would give him a good kicking then call the police –

MICHELE DECOY
Absolutely disgusting, he's a vile piece of shit police should hang their head in shame –

THERESA DECOY
If it was one of there children he would be arrested straight-away. I fully understand why so many people take the law into their own hands when our justice system always fails us disgraceful –

PAM DECOY
Absolutely shocking. That police force should be VERY ashamed of themselves –

MARK HUNTER
Kill all beasts –

DONNA DECOY
Police are fucking useless no wonder people dish out street justice –

When a 27-year-old man in Ireland was acquitted of raping a 17-year-old,[12] word quickly spread that his lawyer had convinced the jury that the girl herself provoked the sexual act by wearing a thong with a lace front. To show the absurdity of this line of reasoning, a Member of Parliament produced a lace thong from her sleeve and held it up for all in the chamber to see. It ignited a myriad of supporting public protests. The MP called the defence yet one more example of 'routine victim-blaming', and inspired women in Ireland to post photographs of underwear in all shapes and sizes using the hashtag #ThisIsNotConsent. Two hundred others marched on the courthouse to place underwear on its steps while, in Dublin, protestors strung a washing line of women's underwear between lampposts. The hunting community was quick to join in. As one decoy put it: 'I could walk round with pierced feckin fanny flaps and a crystal unicorn tail butt plug it don't give any cracker the right to force his dirty member up me spout. Rape is rape and that barrister needs a broken jaw for doing that.' The legal apparatus is, as far as they are concerned, ready for the chop.

It is hard not to feel some sympathy for the police, and not just because they lack sufficient resources to do their job. It is because they are also often the first to witness the brutal reality of sexual abuse. I knew what predators were capable of but hadn't appreciated how they are only the tip of a much bigger iceberg. As a senior New Scotland Yard detective told me, some of what he's seen in the course of his work he hasn't the stomach to describe. Much of it is produced overseas but available for viewing anywhere in the world, including in the UK. He told of children raped before a live audience, selected from whatever 'stock' happened to be available and subjected to whatever abuse viewers were willing to pay for. Videos of children abused by their own older siblings for payment or because they were blackmailed into doing so. Of babies thrown out of buildings and their corpses molested. Nothing is too sordid not to be available on demand for anyone willing to pay for it.

Participation in these online events often requires those new to the site to make and share a first-generation image. That is, the ticket of admission is a photograph or video you have generated yourself, featuring the abuse of a child, that presumably could be held against you should you violate whatever rules are imposed. This helps weed out undercover police who, for legal and ethical concerns wouldn't be able to comply with this requirement (even if new technologies help police manipulate images to enable undercover investigations).

Years later, I still often wonder how all this abuse is even possible: who in their right mind would pay to see those more vulnerable being abused? Who has the stomach for this stuff? And yet, the detective said, any functioning society should be able to show humanity towards even these predators, and especially to those who were once victims of abuse. He then said that one of the problems with hunters live streaming stings is that it pulls the rug out from under those who may have never contemplated taking their own lives but, because of the exposure and humiliation, now do. No matter how bad some of these abusers are, there are those who are genuinely remorseful for what they've done, are ashamed, and want to do better in future, and it is these people we must try to understand and help.

At this he paused. I understood what he was trying to tell me – that the fabric of social life needs compassion and forgiveness if it is not to come loose at the seams – and yet, having just been told how bleak it gets when travelling down the vortex, so much of me simply wishes for predators to burn in hell instead.

9

We're huddling in the parking lot of a Premier Inn not a million miles from Jay and Saz's semi-detached.

'Ugh,' Saz sighs, 'I hate doing stings so close to home. What if anyone recognises us?' She says word will spread and everyone who hates what hunters do will end up making their lives miserable. Jay doesn't mind at all, he says, and would happily light up his own neighbour were he to discover they're having it off with kids.

Saz is the decoy for tonight's target. Seeing as COBRA weren't able to find an address for tonight's suspect, and because the team have enough dirt on him to secure his arrest, they're trying a honeytrap instead. Saz approached him online as a woman interested in consensual casual sex. Should he fall for the trap *and* be seen to use the same WhatsApp number used to groom a child online, we know we have our man, and all bets are off.

By the time our suitor shows up, Saz has already netted herself another man who'd seen her smoking outside the Premier Inn and wondered if she might like to join him inside. Aware of how important it is that she should be seen to be alone so as not to scare off the predator, she dismisses his advances – chuffed, she says later, that she can still 'pull'. When the predator comes into view a few minutes later, Jay and Vince are quick off the mark. Our suspect told Saz that he'd done jail time and now works as a 'sack carrier', which everyone takes to mean that he is big and strong, and Jay wasn't going to take any chances with his wife as bait.

Imagine our surprise then when our predator is slim, polite and obliging, quickly admitting to having tried to groom a real child and appreciative of how professionally we handled it all. It is almost as if we did him a service and, who really knows, one does hear of offenders wishing to be picked up for not being able to stop what they are doing. Is he one of those, I wonder. Or has he simply seen plenty of sting videos online and is grateful that his own exposure wasn't as humiliating and highly charged as it could have been? Or maybe he cottoned onto the fact that nothing de-escalates conflict quite like a quick admission of guilt. The police too are quick to turn up and make the arrest.

The following morning Saz sends me links to three Facebook posts. All, she says, go to show how terrible a place the hunting community can be. By now I've become accustomed to seeing hunters take their grievances out on each other online, and yet the posts unsettle. The first link opens into a heated online argument about a female 'hunter' being 'unmasked' as working undercover for the police. She fiercely denies the charge, as well as a string of other crimes that have no obvious bearing on child abuse but greatly animate her accusers: of being a dog thief, of animal neglect, of selling dodgy puppies to unsuspecting buyers, of taking money from decoys, of reporting a decoy to social services, of online trolling, of distributing revenge porn, of deleting evidence on predators, and of putting hunters' children at risk by identifying them on Facebook. You name it and she's done it.

In a long reply, she disputes all charges though admits having been asked by police to provide details on different paedophile hunting teams – in what geographical areas these teams were active, whether they live streamed or streamed to a secret Facebook group, and what she knew about their membership – but says she never delivered. The hunting community, however, isn't impressed. They threaten to call social services and, if this wasn't enough, to steal her dogs, slit her throat and, more generally, ruin her life. They say they will call on the Samaritans to help them achieve the above, even if it isn't at all obvious to me why. The point is that any betrayal risks being severely punished by the hunting community.

These links, like so many that Saz and Oliver send my way, are like portals into a parallel world: a world free of subtlety, where every situation is simplified, where characters are typical rather than unique and there to set lived experience to a dramatic score. A world adjudicated along straightforward lines: good vs evil, right vs wrong, true vs false, friend vs foe, either/or. And yet is a world that has real consequences for those who happen to fall prey to it.

This challenge is a familiar one for ethnographers who've been around the block, as it is to journalists and those who make a living writing the lives of others. The wonderfully incisive opening to Janet Malcolm's *The Journalist and the Murderer* lays out the problem:

> Every journalist who is not too stupid or full of himself to notice what is going on knows that what he does is morally indefensible. He is a kind of confidence man, preying on people's vanity, ignorance, or loneliness, gaining their trust and betraying them without remorse. Like the credulous widow who wakes up one day to find the charming young man and all her savings gone, so the consenting subject of a piece of nonfiction learns – when the article or book appears – his hard lesson.[1]

For again, what aspects of the lives of strangers do we have the right to publicly expose? When is informed consent truly informed, and what rights to privacy do informants retain once they've given consent? We've already considered unhappy replies from those who featured in Nancy Scheper-Hughes' ethnography of rural Ireland. But there are plenty more where these came from. For example, the protagonist of William Foote Whyte's *Street Corner Society* was so embarrassed by the account, and concerned that others might react badly to it, that he actively discouraged local reading of the book: 'The trouble is, Bill, you caught the people with their hair down. It's a true picture, yes; but people feel it's a little too personal.'[2]

The risk of being accused of betrayal by those who opened their homes to you feels all the more acute where the stakes for informants are high or where they're unusually vulnerable. A classroom example of this is Laud Humphreys' fieldwork in 'tearooms' – slang for public toilets used for impersonal sex between gay men – where Humphreys offered to act as a 'watchqueen' while visitors engaged in fellatio, meaning he volunteered to keep an eye out for police, peering out of (and, as is obvious from his accounts, also in through) a small window.

Humphreys' study was controversial for several reasons. He was accused of not having been clear about his intentions to informants when he used police records to find out who these men were and where they lived (based on the licence plates of the cars they drove). He gained access to the records, having offered to help police administer a health survey, on the understanding that he'd be allowed to add some questions of his own. Many of his informants were surprised to see their 'watchqueen' on their doorstep. He subsequently interviewed these men, even in the presence of their wives, knowing something about them their wives likely did not. But this isn't the primary reason why Humphreys' ethnography is of interest; it is because 'the men in the tearooms couldn't fight back'.[3] His informants were a relatively powerless group, unable or too ashamed to retaliate, and when visited in their own homes were at risk of being outed.

I write to Saz straightaway. I tell her that I hope she knows I'm not a police informer; that I'm not paid by the police and do what I do independent from them; that, as an academic, I do my best to understand what the world looks like from their point of view, how they choose to act within it and how they live their lives on their own terms; that I've extended the same courtesy to the police; that, if all goes well, I might be able to help police and hunters to better understand how they might work alongside each other to keep children safe. I know this makes me sound defensive but how can I not be?

'Lol,' she writes back. 'I never thought you was, Jack. This has just come out and we are all a little confused by it all to be honest. The police say we are corrupt but just shows you they are.' I feel a great sense of relief at her reply. But it also causes me to revisit why it is COBRA took me on board in the first place, and with such good grace, when few other teams would. I remember Jay and Saz telling me on that first night how they'd received similar requests many times – from journos, PhD students, academics – only to turn them down. Perhaps my timing was fortunate, seeing how tired they were of being cast as 'vigilantes' and 'glory hunters' by media and police unwilling to appreciate how different hunting teams are, and how their motives can only really be understood when considering their personal circumstances. I wonder if they know that they themselves are at risk of falling foul of the very same criticism they levy against the police: of 'caricaturing' the other; of refusing to see the particular in the general, of being the pot calling the kettle black.

As I get ready for bed, Jay sends me a video he thinks might be of interest. Its protagonist is a man who sent videos of himself in a state of arousal to a 12-year-old girl. The problem is that this man is a repeat offender who is known to have attended remedial courses to help him with his addiction to porn and his attraction to kids. The father of the girl had discovered the videos and taken them straight to the police but, Jay says, 'police didn't do nothing'. So, he went to a hunting team instead who charged right out to confront the predator in a live-streamed sting. 'Just shows you that if police don't act people come to us.'

'Wow,' I write back.

'Not a good idea to bring the dad along though,' replies Jay.[4]

10

Jay and Saz are keen to show me some examples of 'bad practice' within the hunting community – all part of my training they say – and send along links to a string of online videos. In the first of these, a couple of hunters force a predator to go flat out onto the pavement after he refused to take his hands out of his pockets. Pinning him to the ground, they tell the viewing public that he had only just been released from prison for stabbing someone and so they aren't keen to take their chances. The thing is, one of the hunters is clutching what appear to be 'knuckledusters' and it is this that Jay and Saz take issue with.

'FFS!!' Jay writes.

I then notice that the 'knuckleduster' has given many in the hunting community cause to have their say about the matter. In response, the 'offending' team posts a justification the next day:

> I wish to apologize for the actions of a member of our security. Although the item she had was NOT a knuckle duster, it was in fact a rubber handle for a dog lead ... but that is NO EXCUSE for it to be branded in the way it was. I as team Founder, nor any of my team condone this behaviour. We wish to enable the justice system to deal with these predators in the correct manner. We are NOT vigilantes nor would we support such behaviour. The team member in question is deeply saddened by her actions and regrets what she has done. ... My family work hard at what they do

and we are an honest team, it would not be right for other members to be criticized. We as a team will be taking some time away to reflect and gather ourselves after such a shocking event. But i hope the community will welcome us back and continue to support all the goid work we have done and all we will achieve in the future ... much love and Respect.

I am feeling increasingly intrigued by how much time hunters spend watching each other (online) relative to time spent watching predators. In this respect, they bear an uncanny similarity to 'ultras' in Italian football. As Tobias Jones wrote of his time spent with these ultras: 'weirdly, one of the ways to spot the ultras is that many aren't paying attention to the game ... They are watching the troops. The more long-in-the-tooth ultras work the *curva* like hosts at a party ... Being an ultra isn't about watching the football but watching each other: admiring the carnival on the *curva*, not the game on the grass.'[1]

Watching the carnival may seem wasteful, and particularly if that time could be better spent keeping children safe, but it allows teams like COBRA to learn from the mistakes of others and draw positive comparisons between them and those who are 'in it for the wrong reasons'. So, for example, after a team torched the property of what they thought was a predator, a rival team was quick to post a 'verdict' on Facebook: 'So the vigilante justice idiots are out in Kilmarnock tonight, well done you complete and utter bellends. You realise that the garage you just burned to the ground belonged to another owner and not the predator who was stung today ... you're a bunch of idiots.'

Likewise, the Dark Justice team wrote of their fear about being stigmatised in the media courtesy of teams who seemed to think paedophile hunting as 'some sort of entertainment'. So it seems that by comparing themselves to other teams – in fact a form of moral grandstanding – hunters affirm the moral purity of their practices and stake out their claim of moral superiority over both the authorities and other hunting teams.

Occasionally, this grandstanding produces tensions that then show up in all manner of unpleasantness, as Jay discovered in a message sent him by another hunter: 'I fucking hate you and your slag wife. Your misses is a gin drunken whore begging Jss for coke bring ya karma train I'll smash your in the face with it. Your finished.' Another online post (not by COBRA) flags the case of a predator stung at his home and in the presence of his partner and child. It turns out that the predator and female hunter once were colleagues on the same hunting team, and that now he'd been caught grooming what he believed to be a 13-year-old girl in a wheelchair. The hunter was none the happier for their shared history and wasn't about to do him any favours, and as she grew ever angrier at his unresponsiveness, he shut the door on her. She spent the next two hours on her knees shouting abuse through his letterbox, causing concerned neighbours to eventually call the police to clear up the mess. When the police arrived, they locked her into the stairwell while escorting the suspect out through a service entrance in his apart-ment building. The sting footage meanwhile had gone live and no sooner had the suspect been released on bail than he was given a stiff beating by his neighbours on the housing estate where his apartment building stood.

To do this – to have 'a go' at a predator – is a source of pride for many. One of those involved in the beating admitted as much online, writing that he'd given the predator a 'proper slap and he's going to get one every time I see him'. The predator then took his own grievances to the very same Facebook forum and posted a letter from his solicitor saying that the police decided to take no further action (NFA), even though his solicitor emphasised that this didn't mean the police might not arrest him again for the same offence in future. The female hunter who'd confronted him wrote to say that her team never claimed to be professionals. And also that her team were never wrong.

I don't know if the issue was ever resolved. In fact, I'm rarely ever left with the impression that things are amicably resolved, if resolved at all. Their world, to me at least, still feels mesmerisingly chaotic. And this is precisely what Wolf Pack's Oliver so loves about it – the unashamed, unmitigated aggression of it all – because it exposes a side of our shared humanity that is unaffected by conven-tional etiquette. I now also wonder if many of the videos Saz and Jay send along for me to look at are really designed as a fold for their own stings, showing me how professional COBRA are by comparison.

It is why they will refuse to do a sting if the evidence doesn't stack up, as happened this evening: 'the chat logs came through as pure intrapement,' Saz texted me. 'Morally I'm not going to do it as intrapement and I wouldn't sting unless I'm 100 they are guilty. You don't go destroying people life and their family for fun. Its not a game.'

Later in the week, I meet with a detective sergeant in charge of a small police team tasked with monitoring cases of child sexual abuse. He interacts with paedophile hunters on a regular basis. When I ask him to talk me through his experience with hunters, he seems broadly sympathetic. What he objects to is exposing suspected paedophiles live online (and without affording them an assumption of innocence, which is theirs by right); as to the aggression of some teams, when 'the red mist kicks in, and the shouting starts, and they get caught up in the emotions of it all,' he says. 'If a police officer behaved like that they'd be out of a job.'

He also says that he suspects hunters don't feel that the police are receptive to their work, which, in some cases, he admits they aren't. But then he says that hunters don't understand the processes they must go through if they are to successfully prosecute a suspected predator. He continues:

> My experience of the decoys is that they're very well-intentioned people from anywhere in their twenties to in their seventies doing it because they've got grandchildren. And they don't want these predators doing what they're doing. And the police shouldn't be against that – we should be applauding it. They're increasing in number because we're not doing enough of it, and I understand their frustration. And so I think the decoys taking over conversations from real children are quite good, if you like. But I think the – for lack of a better word – rent-a-mob that they send to the scene are terrible. They are out to embarrass predators as much as they can and then live stream without thinking through the risk to that person there and then and afterwards. For them it's all about the noise and exposure and dramatics.

The job of hunters is to protect children and not to get predators to commit suicide or have their house attacked or them having to move home. Once predators are on the sex offenders register, we much prefer them to be working during the day because at least they're then not sat in front of a computer for eight hours. But these teams put a camera in their face and shout at them for twenty minutes, basically saying, 'you're a paedophile! you're a paedophile!' And obviously the predators aren't going to stand in front of a camera and say, 'yes, I am.' That's just not going to happen. And so, some of them just start shouting more and more and I'm like, 'how's that working for you?' And you know what, when they're being shouted at and are still in the house and start deleting evidence that could have shown that they were part of an organised ring that had abused lots of children, I'm not so sure they'd think their moment of Facebook glory to have been so worthwhile. Or at least I hope they don't.

I ask him whether he'd be happy for decoys to continue doing what they do so long as the evidence is then handed to the police. 'Yes,' he says, 'but on the understanding the CPS [Crown Prosecution Service] will cooperate and do their utmost to get a prosecution.' He tells me that part of the problem is that the CPS are making prosecutions of this type of offence almost impossible, so it's no real surprise that decoys feel like 'oh, we handed it to police, and nothing happens'. The police really do try to get to the point of charging the predator but are often told that there isn't enough corroborating evidence. The CPS don't believe that the chat they are given hasn't been edited and so they will often ask for the phone used to generate the chat to be handed over, which raises all sorts of difficulties for decoys. 'If it's a decoy in Manchester talking to somebody in Hertfordshire, the practicalities of seizing that phone are not straightforward. And then decoys will be like "I'm not giving up this phone. I'm speaking to ten suspects on this phone, and not just your suspect." And I appreciate that, and I think it's appalling that the CPS don't take what the police say or receive from a member of the public in the best intentions.'

I say this must be frustrating. 'It is!' he says.

I've got 26 years in the police now. If a decoy provides a statement that says, 'I have handed every communication and everything I have to police,' that is a statement; that's a lawful document. Why is it anybody's place to disbelieve that? It's gone from trying to prosecute people to finding reasons to not. And I'm sure there are some corrupt decoys, the same as there are some corrupt police officers – that's life – but 99.9% of these people are not what the press depicts them to be.

Changing tack, I ask him how he and his team cope with facing up daily to so much depravity. He tells me they joke around a fair bit, which helps. They also have access to counselling, though that's gotten worse over the years.

When it first started up, it was very good and well-intentioned but now it's just pathetic. They don't have time. They don't give us an appointment when we need it. We had one girl have a mental breakdown at work and so we immediately rang occupational health, and they told us they could see her in three weeks' time.

And now we get an email once a year with a form with one of the questions saying, 'Do you feel suicidal?' I mean, Christ! Seriously?

Back home, I find yet another sting video in my inbox and a brief note from Saz saying that 'this the worst one I believe and one day a predator will take his life'. I sit down to watch the spectacle. A team from northern England stung a man they believed to have been talking online to an 11-year-old girl. When they told him who they were and what they were there to do, he did a runner. But the hunters were quick on their feet, tackled him and dragged him by his armpits onto a park bench, where he was closely watched by the team's security detail. Just as they were about to start questioning him, the one in charge looked at his watch and told the predator that because he'd done a runner, they'd nearly missed Armistice Day's two-minute silence, an annual tradition that always takes place at 11am on the 11th day of the 11th month. And so the hunter called for a two-minute silence right there and then, ordering the suspect to 'show respect, you bastard!'. But of course the suspect availed himself of the opportunity to do another runner.

He's quickly caught and physically restrained. He is also told that his sting is being viewed live by 5,000 people and that because his face is now 'out there', even if he got bailed someone might recognise him and beat the living daylights out of him. As if that wasn't enough, they tell him that when he is finally thrown in prison, he'll be 'the bitch' on the wing. Of course, whether any of it comes to pass is bye-the-bye insofar as this is all part entertainment.

I'm by no means the only one to spot the absurdity of it all. The online community is already in full swing:

CLARISSA DECOY

Three teams carrying out two stings on armistice day [...] on the 11th hour of the 11th day, one of those two paedophiles stung is asked to respect the two minute silence whilst he is being restrained. I really couldn't make this shit up even if I tried lol. It seems that no matter how special or important a day is meant to be the hunters can't even give it a rest for one flaming day, or at the very least, carry the sting out in the evening. I guess when the queen pops her clogs and it's the day of her funeral, it will be the same thing –

LUKE HUNTER

I used to quite enjoy these paedophile hunter videos but now with groups like predator exposure who just create drama and use their numbers and uneducated gobs to intimidate the accused person. Quite uncomfortable to watch, makes them just as low as the paedophiles like –

TRACEY DECOY

What the actual fuck? Is it possible to get as low as a paedophile? If u don't like wot u see then don't watch, simple –

KATE DECOY

Would look into that one what a prick –

ELLEN DECOY

Who cares what way a paedophile is spoken to, didn't they lose their rights when they started abusing kids –

LINSEY DECOY
Intimidate them? I'd do more than intimidate them. Ignore
these trolls. You guys are amazing –

PAMELA DECOY
Different if it was his kids getting groomed –

DENISE DECOY
Luke ain't got a clue and is a paedophile simpathiser –

MIKE HUNTER
Luke, you sad person, in my book anything that keeps
children safe is good –

JASON HUNTER
What an absolute bell-end. He's probably one himself –

11

While paedophile hunting wouldn't exist if not for online predators, I suspect that the persistence of a small core of teams has less to do with a steady inflow of new predators than with the opportunity they offer for people to build and sustain social bonds. For example, while a sting can take anywhere from 20 minutes to 4 hours (with the average time probably being around under an hour), the overall affair can easily take up an entire evening. This is because a disproportionate amount of time is spent socialising. Having decided to meet up at a McDonald's near to the suspect's location – or, when there isn't a McDonald's nearby, then a supermarket – hunters take time to reconnect over a meal or drinks. The ostensible reason for meeting beforehand is to brief the team on important details that surfaced from the recce, even if these briefs take at most a few minutes each. Then, once a sting is 'in the bag', the team heads back to a fast-food joint or pub to continue what they started earlier that day, and it's not unusual for two consecutive stings on a Saturday or Sunday to take up all day.

It isn't that safeguarding children by getting predators offline and off the streets isn't important – it is – but that so much of what preoccupies conversations within COBRA appears geared towards social bonding. Perhaps this comes with the territory: hunting peadophiles is emotionally so affecting that support systems are particularly vital. It is also likely that a focus on child sexual abuse tends to attract survivors keen to make sure that what happened to them does not happen to anyone else.

Jane Hunter: *Thanks for all your support guys*♥[1]

Mike Hunter: We *are all here for you we are family and look out for each other and support when necessary*

This social side of COBRA also shows up in its private chatrooms, of which the busiest by far have little or nothing to do with hunting per se. Instead, it covers all and sundry: everyday activities and hobbies, television, politics and global affairs, and personal issues around family, jobs, and very often, health. Even considering the Covid-19 pandemic, the scarcity of discussion about victims remains surprising. While it is understandable that suspected predators are central to the group's discussions, it is much less clear why victims are so peripheral to it. It may be that the group largely operates using decoys and so real victims are almost never involved. It is also possible that it is taken as a given that real victims are central to the group's cause and so do not require any further justification. The real child, in other words, remains some-what of an abstraction.

Chats are also conspicuously affective insofar as COBRA hunters treat each other as close friends or family members might, even if they rarely meet face-to-face, and nor does it take long for novices to become the object of affection. When I joined in October 2018, I imagined it might take a while for hunters to take a liking to me, or if that's too high a bar then at least be comfortable having me around. For all I know this may well have been the case. Yet every indication – the use of affective prose and emojis in con-versations directed at me – told me otherwise: they suggested that I was meant to feel like I was one of them right from the get-go. It may be that Saz and Jay did a good job preparing the team for my presence – they at the very least will have explained who I was and what I was here to do – but I was never made to feel like an outsider. I was grateful for them not minding me hanging around and would of course tell them who I was and who I was with and what I was here to do. But all it ever took was for me to be vouched for by one of their own. The hunters I got to know were hard-working mums and dads who didn't necessarily have the best start in life but got on with it; people who care about others and what others think of them; people who may be politically conservative but liberally minded when it comes to sexual and gender preference, the casual use of marijuana and to ethnic diversity. Like many, they too wish for a better, fairer world.

But affections can change and can do so quickly and dramatically following violations of team etiquette or because of within-team quibbles. One sees this reflected in contributions from the watching public, whose support for hunters and disdain for predators nearly always finds expression in the strongest possible terms. In fact, this online support leaves one with the distinct impression that hunters enact the grievances of a broader community from which they also take their mandate. It is something hunters are acutely aware of. For example, when I was occasionally asked to hold the recording device to live stream a confrontation between hunters and predator, expressions of affection (typically using heart emojis), or of anger towards the suspect, liberally scrolled across the smartphone from the 2,000 to 4,000 online viewers,[2] many of whom see this as more than entertainment: they are willing participants in a public spectacle of humiliation; they endorse the pursuit of justice, even revenge, by those more courageous or more mobile for which they offer a protective fold. They make sure hunters know they're not alone; that there are others who would have their back and might have been there too if circumstances were different.

Many hunters also see themselves as gatekeepers of their teams. I remember Oliver telling me how the car ride to our sting venue had been carefully orchestrated, and that I wasn't the only newbie to join Wolf Pack that day; a rough-at-the-edges looking 20-something in jogging pants and a hoodie had asked to join the team and been invited along. He'd told Oliver that he had grown up on a local housing estate. It so happened that it was the same estate one of the other Wolf Pack lads grew up in. The problem was that Wolf Pack hadn't ever even heard of this new face nor seen him around on the estate. That doesn't make sense, Oliver told me, because 'on these estates, everyone knows everyone'. So, a decision was made for one of Wolf Pack's own to accompany this novice on our car journey to the predator's flat, 'to suss him out like'.

This affective disposition is vulnerable to abuse. I remember Oliver telling me about one team member who prided himself on having been in the SAS and, one day, wrote in the team chat that he needed to take some time off hunting because his daughter had killed herself. Every hunter and decoy rallied around online to express their sympathies and to offer help. He then posted another message to say that his mum had died as well and, again, everyone wrote in to express their heartfelt sorrow and how can it be that disaster strikes twice and within such a short window of time. People ended up sending flowers and gifts to his address only to have them returned because he wasn't known at that address. After a few days of this, the team find out that none of what he said was true: his daughter hadn't killed herself, his mum hadn't died, and the SAS had never heard of him. He'd made it all up. Once the team found out, their affections understandably turned into a deep dislike, disgusted that someone would lie about these things and make everyone else out to be fools.

While Wolf Pack and COBRA enjoy a good working relationship, Jay and Saz have been known to refuse to execute stings on Wolf Pack's behalf if the evidence appeared sketchy. A recent one of these involved a predator in the southeast of London, who'd been talking to one of Wolf Pack's decoys. Jay felt the decoy had been edging the conversation on beyond what any ordinary child could be expected to say and figured this wasn't one for them. As Oliver told me,

> We offered it to COBRA because we didn't think he was gonna come up to Glasgow, but they wouldn't take it off us. They felt it was a bit too leading and it was our decoy's first chat log, and so we thought, well he's still chatting to us and if he's going to come up all the way from Kent to us on a bus as a 50-year-old to meet a 14-year-old, then we thought, Fuck him. So, we waited at the bus stop with a 'Welcome to Scotland' sign and picked him out straightaway, and as soon as we did, he soiled himself, and then we had to sit with him until police arrived.

'Turns out,' Oliver says, 'that he'd been to prison for eight years already for pulling a 14-year-old off a horse and trying to rape her. We looked him up on the internet afterwards and his life was just so grubby; there's just something about him that's so earthy, so Fred West. Police ended up putting him in prison.'

I ask Oliver how it is that as an openly gay man from a middle-class English family he seems so at home among hunters from rough estates and with prison time under their belts. He tells me that he decided long ago to work his way down the social ladder if only to spite his own family. He hadn't much interest in bettering himself, he said, but did crave for a place where life felt more authentic, closer to the bone, and saw hunting as the activists' equivalent of architectural brutalism: big and honest and unpretentious.

Logging into my Facebook account, I notice a new message from Saz. She wonders if I have seen the news: that three male and two female members of Predator Exposure have been arrested by West Yorkshire Police, and isn't this another example of some teams giving other teams a bad name? I click on the embedded link. It tells me that Predator Exposure have been accused of false imprisonment, assault and public order offences, relating to a sting on 11 August 2018 in Wakefield and 13 January 2019 in Leeds. I watch one of the stings on Facebook. In it, a predator seeks refuge in a corner shop after having done a runner to rid himself of hunters. Undeterred, the team enter the shop and drag him out of it to continue the interrogation where they left off. One of the predator's shoes came off in the scuffle. Whether the shop owner or predator filed a complaint, or whether it was a member of the public or police watching the sting footage, the hunters were arrested and bailed and are now awaiting a court appearance. The news of the arrests has triggered an outpouring of sympathy for Predator Exposure and a video response from their leader, Phil Hoban:

> Fuck West Yorkshire police. They're a pile of shite. We've reported it to you and we're still waiting eight months later, the dirty bastard is still speaking to us. So this is why we don't hand the evidence over to you, so do what you're fucking doing because this is the bottom fucking line; at the end of the day you're not doing enough, and we told you before. Suck my fucking balls, that all I can say.

12

Saz and I crouch behind a black Ford Focus in a string of parked cars in a 1960s housing development in East Anglia. She is feeling mischievous, as am I, in what feels like an adult version of hide-and-seek. We look at each other and giggle. Two others are hunkering behind a big bush with another two tucked in behind a garden wall. Jay and Steve sit tucked in behind a car near ours but much nearer Lindsey's silver sedan. Lindsey's been a decoy with COBRA for a couple of years and, unlike other decoys, regularly joins us on stings.

Our suspect has been talking to Wolf Pack's Oliver (decoying as a 14-year-old boy) and so tonight's sting is executed on behalf of our Scottish friends. Seeing how they are based in Glasgow, and the predator is 350 miles south of the Scottish border, Oliver asked Jay and Saz to light this one up. There's some urgency to tonight's sting as the suspect lives with his partner and her son who, coincidentally, is nearly the same age as Oliver's decoy.

Jay wrote last night to ask if I were free to join them on the hunt.

JAY HUNTER
Jack are you free tomorrow night in your area –

ME
Sure –

JAY HUNTER
It's for Wolf Pack as well mate –

ME
Where shall I meet you –

SAZ DECOY
Ok guys we need to look for address, although WP will try for meet. Oliver can you add chat logs in hear as won't let me babe xx

OLIVER BRAID
Absolutely. We're also sort of dreaming of coming down for it because Wolf Pack's bail conditions are only for Scotland ha ha, plus it means we can all do it together. But otherwise we're more than happy for you guys to get him. I'll just check with people up here to see if we can realistically make it, but otherwise totally yes let's just get him tucked away –

LINDSEY DECOY
Ok we will see what Jay thinks what time and days would be better and we will set something up. Let us know if your peeps prefer a certain day to make it down xx

OLIVER BRAID
Okay so we think it is too far for us to drive. But it means you guys can just go for him! I'm going to update the log and add my MG11 in then you should be good –

JAY HUNTER
That's a damn shame guys as would love to finally meet you all –

OLIVER BRAID
I'm going to try to build a story for how I'd be in that area. If he doesn't go for it lets just grab him. I think he's so gross –

LINDSEY DECOY
Jay I sent you an advert . . . he is selling exotic beards . . . I can pretend that Im getting them for my bro who kept them for years xx

JAY HUNTER
Call u later I gotta plan –

LINDSEY DECOY
Ok well he wants to sell me two dragons. And he will guide me on what sex –

OLIVER BRAID
Amazing!

LINDSEY DECOY
He sounds like a right DRIP –

JAY HUNTER
Lets run some checks on the address and then were good to go –

OLIVER BRAID
Thanks dude, let's get this drip in the bin –

SCOTT HUNTER
Got a picture of his house from google maps. Very big house for one guy unless he has 500 dragons –

SAZ DECOY
No way he lives alone –

OLIVER BRAID
IU ... had such a caravan/bedsit vibe from him. Parents house? I be bowled over if he's married –

LINDSEY DECOY
He has agreed to me getting the dragons tomorrow between 7–8 pm –

OLIVER BRAID
Pretty sure this is him on FB. Btw he hasn't spoken to me at all today so if you guys are up for tomorrow that would be amazing –

LINDSEY DECOY
He don't look like how his voice sounds –

OLIVER BRAID
Omg check out his wall, he's selling so much shit, dolls houses, mini trucks, sofas –

LINDSEY DECOY
Imagine if Phil Hoban gets jail time and he has to share it with a nonce –

SCOTT HUNTER
Saz what time do you expect to go live –

SAZ DECOY
About 19.30 xx

SCOTT HUNTER
Ok cool . . . stay safe –

Lindsey walks up the garden path to the suspect's house and rings the bell. Jay, Steve, Saz and I meanwhile have eyes on the front door while all the other hunters have eyes on us. Our predator opens to see a smiling Lindsey and nothing in his demeanour suggests he suspects her to be anything other than another enthusiast. Wearing jeans and Metallica t-shirt, heavy-set and with a scruffy beard, he appeared to be in his late thirties. He shouts something indistinct to someone else in the house before he closes the door behind him and follows Lindsey to her car.

'It's in the boot,' she tells him.

He's fallen for the hustle. Saz and I watch him follow Lindsey and, just as she's about to open the boot to her car, Jay and Steve appear from behind a nearby vehicle and block his way back into the house. Jay carries a manilla folder with 110 printed pages of screenshots of chats between the predator and a '14-year-old boy'. I carry Jay's paedo-pack on my back.

It's clear that he hasn't the foggiest idea of the trouble he is in. Might they have a word with him, they ask, and as they begin their interrogation, the rest of us resurface from our hiding places and encage him.[1] Fifteen minutes into the interrogation I do what is now my role in the team: I phone the police to make the arrest. Giving the officer on the other end of the line my name, I tell her that I am part of a child protection team (COBRA never uses the term 'paedophile hunters' in relation to the police), then give her the name of the predator and our location. She tells me the police will be on their way shortly. Meanwhile, the predator's partner has stepped out of the house wondering what all the kerfuffle is about. Saz intercepts her and tells her who we are and what we are here to do. She appears shocked to be told that her partner had sent sex videos to a boy only two years older than her own son.

'Where's your son now?' Saz asks.

'Upstairs. In his bedroom,' the woman says.

'Maybe make sure he's okay?'

Police arrive in a van and two female officers get out. The sergeant in charge isn't at all happy to see us and makes no effort at disguising her contempt.

'You're VIGILANTES,' she shouts from across the road and loud enough for all and sundry to hear. 'You have no business whatsoever doing what you're doing,' she says, and repeats the name-calling several times over. Predictably, the accusation is about as well received as can be expected. Saz tells her that if the police only did their job there wouldn't be any reason for us to do any of this, and then says they tried handing police the evidence many times in the past but that the police don't act and so what do they expect.

The sergeant isn't about to back down, and nor is Saz, and the result is a face-off that is attracting the attention of neighbours. The police sergeant keeps repeating that COBRA are 'vigilantes', which infuriates the hunters. Saz retorts by saying COBRA aren't vigilantes at all and that, 'by the way', they have at least twice as much experience as police do with this sort of thing. The sergeant turns her attention to Jay and tells him he shouldn't be interviewing the predator without placing him 'under caution' and that he has now compromised the entire case and is wasting police time.

'Go home,' she says, 'and enjoy the glory of hunting.' Jay asks her why she is being so snarky seeing they've done all the hard work and all that's left is to make the arrest.

'Oh really,' she replies, 'maybe I should arrest all of you too and get you to hand over your phones.'

It is the first time I've seen a police officer tell hunters to their faces that they are vigilantes and have no place in fighting crime. Such criticisms only firm up the resolve of COBRA, who treat them as confirmation that the police and the judiciary cannot be relied on to protect children. It also seems to me that tonight's disjointedness is a pocket version of a much broader challenge nationally, where paedophile hunters and law enforcement are locked in a standoff that prevents a productive conversation in society around how to best combat the insidious and escalating threat of child sexual abuse. One reason for this deadlock may well be the absence of any interest in subtlety and nuance when it comes to exploring the world as experienced by the other: of the complexly interrelated issues that mobilise hunters; of the corresponding policing challenge of having to triage more cases than resources allow; of having to do so with incomplete information and strict legal limits to what police can and cannot do, and talk about. Yet, without such insight, there is a real risk that hunters remain beyond the reach of police and others impacted by their activities.

What is clearly not helping is to frame 'activists' as 'vigilantes'. While the police now formally refrain from doing so (calling them 'Online Child sexual abuse and exploitation Activist Groups' or OCAGs), many in the media are still quick to use the label. Jay, Saz and others within the hunting community take offence at a label they think signifies a 'lack of professionalism' or the very thing they believe they are not. It is why they work so hard to get evidence packs right, to never be physically or verbally abusive towards predators, to carefully vet novice hunters, and why they impose such strict rules on their members on not publicly criticising other teams or stoking unrest from within. The label is an insult, they think, to the effort they invest in taking predators offline and off our streets and to do so (mostly) lawfully. To view vigilantism as synonymous with amateurism also explains why some hunters, Wolf Pack's Oliver included, take great pride in the label, and why the label is used extensively within the hunting community itself to differentiate professionals from amateurs and to condemn those using violence or the threat of violence, reading out excerpts from chat logs to humiliate predators or embarrass them by asking them to perform tricks or sing songs in the false hope that it gets them off the hook.

If the vigilante label isn't helpful, is it necessarily accurate either, as COBRA's agenda is effectively that of the state: both aim to keep children safe. Their ability to do so relies heavily on the police and the judiciary to do their bit: to follow through on the evidence provided. This leaves us in a paradoxical situation, namely that the hunters' success relies on the strength, responsiveness and legitimacy of the very institutions whose perceived impotence confers them their legitimacy.[2,3]

Back at Saz's, Jay invites me into their 'office'. He wants to show me, he says, how easy it is to pick up predators online. I pull up a chair as he loads a social media site called Chat Avenue, where I watch him create a fake profile called 'amy11 f.' He writes 'hi'. Within 90 seconds, he has five replies. One of these features a photograph of a penis along with, 'like what you see?' He tells me that the site features a warning that paedophiles aren't allowed on it and will be taken off straightaway, but says that he's seen no evidence whatsoever of this policy being taken seriously. But swearing is taken seriously, he says, then asking me whether I don't think that strange, and telling me the site is run by paedophiles who kick out anyone they worry might use the site to expose them.

I watch him being booted off the social media site.

'There you go,' he says, 'that's how corrupt they are.'

It turns out that our 'exotic pet' predator was given a long prison sentence, suggesting that he had done far more than 'just' talk dirty to a boy online. Otherwise, it is unlikely that he would have received a custodial sentence rather than a community service order and his name added to the sex offenders' register. Saz and Jay are sure the police discovered that he had been fiddling his partner's son. So that's that.

You never can tell.

13

I wake up to a string of Facebook messages, each of which is a direct response to a single post. The post featured a photograph of David Bibby, 53, from Sale in Greater Manchester, who'd been arrested for participating in an online event where men watch boys under four being raped. Mr Bibby admitted to all charges, was given a three-year community order and ordered to complete fifty days of rehabilitation activity. It hardly needs saying by this point that the online public are less than impressed at what they feel is a slap on the wrist:

'These beasts need tied up n set on fire not given sympathy for the shit going on in their life and a slap on the wrist. No wonder people keep offending,' one of them says. Another writes that it is a 'fucking disgrace' and 'Jail the fucker watching it is the same as doing it' and 'Give me a gun and one bullet' and 'will never understand people getting away with shit like this'.

Yet others have more conspiratorial views: 'System is corrupt ran by elite nonce rings. They seek to normalise this behaviour so sentencing is soft. Why do you think police is now cracking down on leading hunting groups?' and 'Some elite group I reckon and he's a member and so is the judge . . . why is it victim get the life sentence and abusers get the meal ticket??'

'They're in on it for sure,' Jay says, and Saz agrees.

Another Facebook post involves a predator against whom no further action was taken by police despite several decoys submitting evidence of sexual grooming. What's more, he'd been talking to a real child too. The CPS returned the case for lack of evidence, the detective in charge of the case told hunters. He said they could send the case back to the CPS but preparing it for resubmission would require such a long list of tasks to be completed that it could take his team months and with no real prospect of it leading to prosecution. This is what he wrote in a letter posted online:

> I had to face the stark prospect of spending most of the rest of my police service trying to obtain all the microscopic bits and pieces to the exclusion of all other investigations current and future – that simply was not possible. So we then considered the second stark task of whether we 'draw stumps' at that point as the likely sentence he would get in no way came close to the excessive abstraction of staff to obtain it (almost like a 'profit and cost' equation) [...] I feel that the reviewing lawyer simply created such a ridiculous task list just so they wouldn't have to deal with it. In case you haven't seen the latest developments, disclosure and excessive investigation are currently a hot political topic in sexual offence investigations so no lawyer will want to be associated with one that they are worried has a potential hole in the investigation. Therefore they go 'risk averse' and require everything to the nth degree. We are having similar demands with regards allegations of sexual assault and rape, which is serving to totally gum up the investigations and cause major resourcing problems with social services, education and health [...] Sorry if this has come across as a bit of a moan, but as you can see, I am not particularly happy about it either, but that is the reality that we were faced with. Another case may get a different lawyer and a different view, but that will have to be for a different job. Hope this hasn't disheartened you too much, this does not reflect on your guys.[1]

'Shocked and disgusted by this,' one reader replies.

'Bloody work shy and can't be bothered and as long as not my kid I could not care less tosser,' wrote another.

'For all those who say leave it to police see what happens shocking,' says a third, followed by others:

'Totally fucked up what this supposed "people protector" has done!! I hope he is lit up like a bonfire and gets famous for all the wrong reasons!!'

There are more. Many more. But I think I get the gist.

14

'That's him, I'm sure of it,' Lindsey says as she steps into the morning chill, stiff from the car journey, as we all are, and, like us, excited. Outside it's a beautiful early spring morning. Nigel, our suspect, will have driven his family sedan forty-five minutes eastwards to meet what he thinks is a fellow adult for casual sex at a roadside restaurant. What he doesn't know is that one of Lindsey's fellow decoys, Stacey, has been the '12-year-old girl' he'd spent weeks grooming online.

Ordinarily, we might have waited for Nigel to arrange to meet the '12-year-old' in private or to confront him at his home and get him arrested. However, our recent experience with local law enforcement in the arrest of the 'exotic pet' suspect had left many of the team deeply upset. Plus, according to Saz, local police had failed to act on evidence provided by COBRA on a similar case and so we decide to lure Nigel to an adjacent jurisdiction instead, using Lindsey as an adult decoy. Lindsey has earned herself a nickname – 'widow-maker' – for reasons I'm not sure I understand, or at least I don't yet.

He turns left off the main road and into the parking lot, oblivious to five hunters packed in and around a white hatchback outside the diner's entrance, who watch him as he navigates a mostly empty parking lot before settling on a bay furthest from the entrance. We'd arrived in separate cars a good while before the sting and, seeing as we only ever met up for occasions like these, enjoyed the pre-sting banter. Something feels a little naughty about these pre-sting meets: we know something someone else doesn't, and the reason we know is because we choreographed all of it. We have the temporal advantage: we know how this will end whereas he does not, and so while we work backwards from a foregone conclusion, he can only move forward into an uncertain – if for him still tantalising – future. So we gear ourselves up for what is to come, the tell-tale sign of our presence a fairy-ring of cigarette ends. There wasn't any anger, or not yet there, but instead a sense of camaraderie – us against evil – and the piss-take that masked a distinct nervousness. For while we know the outcome, we don't know how our suspect will react when confronted. Jay, in sweats and trainers, gathers the pack as Nigel switches off the engine.

Nigel is 'a bad 'un, a monster and a slaphead nonce that needs gone,' Lindsey had said, and the rest agreed. We had seen his chat logs with the '12-year-old' and they left little doubt about his intentions. Nigel's description of his granddaughter's body raised suspicions that he molested her too, making the team all the more eager to get him offline and behind bars. 'Just pray to god that he ain't touched one them gran kids. But I have a wary feeling. I will stab that fuck in the face if he has I not kidding,' Lindsey had said.

'This shitty life we had isn't an audition,' Jay tells us. 'Be proud and enjoy what we do because, guys, it's good, very good. We save kids.' A knowing nod all round and off we go to meet our target.

'Omg he is so screwed,' Lindsey texts the rest of the COBRA team back home as we set our sights on Nigel who, meanwhile, has gotten out of his vehicle and tugged the discomfort of an hour's drive from his trousers. Had he the slightest inkling of what was in store, he'd have done a runner. Instead, this grandfather of eight calmly fishes a packet of cigarettes from his pocket and lights up, surveying the parking lot up to the restaurant and, beyond it, to a petrol station. With his mind made up, he walks in our direction, not latching on to the fact that we are heading straight for him.

'Excuse me,' Jay says as Nigel's about to walk past us. These first few moments are precious: as Nigel's mind works overtime trying to figure out whether we are law enforcement or not, he is pliable and compliant. Vince asks Nigel if he wouldn't mind following us to a semi-enclosed area out of patrons' view to answer a few questions. In all likelihood Nigel very much minded but he follows instructions regardless, perhaps thinking that privacy may be the only bone thrown his way today. To afford discretion for child predators during interrogations may seem curious given that the affair is streamed live on Facebook to thousands behind keyboards ready for a spectacle, but it's there to shield predators from passers-by who may wish to join in and have a go.

'Stay safe' is the usual chorus from the team back home, even though Nigel hasn't a chance in hell. Pinned in by a picket fence on two sides, we encage him.

'You blocking me in?' Nigel says and, pointing at the smartphone, 'hope you're not taping this'. He shifts uncomfortably when shown a photo of himself and asked if the mug is his. This is followed by a smaller photo of a smaller person: is this the 12-year-old girl he's been grooming online? Nigel says he thought she was 18.

'People lie,' he tells us. Anyone can be anybody online and how was he to know? That the girl had been methodical, telling him three times early on that she was only 12, made not the slightest bit of difference.

I wonder, how is it that the likes of Nigel come to inhabit a world where everything can be denied or twisted: where what is real is what's imagined into being? Where grown-ups can be kids or nurses or firemen and, when under the protective cover of a VPN, can shed all inhibitions in a no-holds-barred, vacuous Wonderland and, when that euphoria wears off, skulk the web for new highs? The technology on which they rely cuts both ways, of course: on the one hand, the internet affords anonymous, low-budget access to pornography of such variety and scale as to make *120 Days of Sodom* seem naive while allowing access to real kids in real time. On the other, this same technology allows hunters to create fake profiles to snare predators – a valuable affordance in that using real kids as bait is morally reprehensible – and then 'out' these predators in front of a live online audience. This audience, in turn, provides hunters with affirmation and a democratic mandate to do more of the same.

Persistent out-and-out denials of any and all charges levelled help bring about a world less sure-footed: where nothing is reliably real, and where everything is adulterated. It is a world not dissimilar to that described by Jonathan Freedland, in experience if not in content, as he recounts listening to David Irving repeatedly deny the Holocaust during a High Court trial by discrediting any evidence of it – witnesses and perpetrators were unreliable, too little remained of the scene of the crime, documents from the period were forgeries –

picturing a world where nothing, no evidence, can be trusted, no matter how compelling. 'It took me a while to understand what this feeling was,' Freedland wrote afterwards. 'But slowly I understood it as a physiological reaction to the world Irving was showing us – a world where nothing was certain, where nothing was firm or solid, where even the most basic facts were in doubt';[1] a world without morals or limits, where we can no longer draw conclusions from the evidence we once thought plainly in view and that, as a matter of fact, remains tucked under Jay's arm as printouts of his online activities. Nigel couldn't give a tinker's cuss.

Jay gets impatient when inquiring into Nigel's motives.

'Why'd you do it?' As is so often the case with predators, Nigel doesn't offer any justification. Whether he really doesn't know or prefers not to say is anyone's guess.

'You haven't been talking to any other children?' Jay says.

'I don't know,' Nigel says.

'You don't know?' Jay says incredulously. Nigel isn't keen to talk.

But Jay doesn't care: 'You don't send images like that to children!'

'And you don't offer to give them a bath neither!' Vince says.

Taking on my usual responsibility, I phone the police. They don't take long to pull up. As Lindsey briefs the officers, Jay tells Nigel that he'll be arrested but won't be harmed.

'What's this if not harming me? You've fucked my life up,' Nigel says.

'You've done that yourself,' Jay replies.

'Now I'm gonna be arrested for being a paedophile.'

'That's what you are,' says Jay, and leaves the matter to the police.

It's been a cool bright morning, and as the sun pushes upwards, we set out for our second sting of the day. Jay hitches a ride with me as we drive twenty miles up in the direction of Lincolnshire. Our second suspect is a single father of four, which has Saz worried. What if the children are in the house with him? How will we safeguard them while securing the exposure and arrest of their dad? It isn't ever a nice thing for kids to see police remove their father and so a plan is hatched to lead the father away from the house and into a nearby cornfield, past three parallel rows of 1930s terraces that feel out of place in this agricultural landscape. Before starting the interrogation, they will tell him he's going to be arrested and instruct him to call a member of the family to come and collect the kids out of sight. That way they can give the man some privacy for the interrogation and spare his kids the humiliation.

Jay and Vince knock on a mid-terrace door and an upstairs window promptly opens.

'Hello,' goes a voice from on high. Looking up, Jay tells him who we are and what we're here to do and, oh yes, could he call a family member to come and pick up whatever kids are in the house as they're going to want to have a chat without his kids being around. The man, in his early forties, puts up no resistance, doesn't even seem all that surprised, calls his mum and joins us outside. As Jay and Vince walk him past his neighbours into an adjacent field, it's clear that prying others would love a bit of the action. Curtains are pulled to the side for a better look. One or two have stepped outside and, if it weren't for us avoiding eye contact, they'd have engaged us in conversation, wondering what was happening on their turf.

Then something I've not seen before happens. The predator begins to shake uncontrollably.

'He's going into shock,' Saz says, and tells him to sit down while asking Jay to lend him his jacket.

'We're not here to hurt you,' she says, 'you're safe with us.' When he asks her what will happen to his children, she says she doesn't know but that social services will want to get involved and she's sure they'd look after them.

As I watch him sitting on damp soil with his arms around his knees and rocking back and forth, I find myself getting nauseous. I know, as Jay and Saz do too, that he's done wrong but – fuck it – how can this be right? Why not give him a right telling off with a warning that all evidence is kept on file in case he tries something like it again, and leave it at that? I mean, he made no effort to meet the decoy face to face, and there is no evidence to suggest he is abusing his own children. How then can it be right to separate him from them by getting social services involved?

An older woman meanwhile pulls up in a small hatchback, wearing a bathrobe over a nightgown and slippers. She has a go straightaway at freshly arrived police. If they go ahead and arrest her son, it means she'll have another four kids to look after, and who is going to pay for all that? And how does any of this have anything to do with her anyways? One of the neighbours walks up to us, the first of several more, and tells us she knows the predator's an alcoholic. She says all the neighbours have always thought him shifty and so she wants to know what he's done. Saz tells her she can't really say. Jay seems to have no such concern, telling the various people now gathered to look up COBRA's Facebook page in a little bit because that would tell them all they need to know. Even if the suspect is bailed tonight, as if often the case, what hope really is there that he'll be able to return to his home without fear of stigmatisation or reprisal now that everyone knows?

In contrast to our first sting today, this one should have been straightforward: the predator owned up to what he'd done and no sooner had he dropped his defences than Saz, Jay and Vince's attitude changed from being accusatory to being reassuring, telling him that help is available for 'people like him'. That way, they say, all this will blow over in no time, even if the online sting video makes that unlikely. As we walk back to our cars, even Saz and Jay admit that this, the sting just now, was a tough one emotionally. I quietly wonder if that means 'morally' too.

Nigel, our first sting that day, is released on bail early Monday morning. On Sunday, and prior to his release, Saz and Jay receive a message from a member of his family.

FAMILY MEMBER
Can you please remove the video of Nigel . . . please think of his wife, children and grandchildren . . . please, I'm begging you –

JAY
Do you mean the guy who said his wife passed away four years ago, said he has abused members of his family, came to meet an adult for a bit of fun . . . also sent pics of animals to a 12-year-old . . . that one –

FAMILY MEMBER
Who has he said that to?

JAY

We have it all documented, and so do the police –

FAMILY MEMBER

Okay please remove it –

JAY

I'm very sorry but this man is a serious predator –

FAMILY MEMBER

I get that but please think of his family. They haven't done anything wrong. I now need your help to protect my mum and my children please –

Her request falls on deaf ears.[2]

A message from someone close to Nigel's family follows a day after his release:

Hi guys. I've been told you conducted a sting on a man called Nigel. I am interested as he was _____. I say was as he committed suicide . . . I'm not berating you guys (you did us all a favour) cuz one of the brothers would have done time if they had found out . . . Thanks for all the hard work you guys do. And if you're ever in the area again there would be a hot drink and a bacon buttie here.

Saz is first to reply, saying how sorry she is for the family that he chose to take his own life, and that this isn't what COBRA is about. She says the team are struggling with events and that they'd taken down the sting video in respect for his family. The family member tells her that he chose to take his life because he was a coward, and not to blame herself or the team. He was a disgusting individual, she says, and tells Saz they're doing a fantastic thing keeping these guys in the public eye. 'I feel for his children,' she signs off, 'they didn't deserve a father like that.'

My own reaction to news of the suicide surprises me insofar that I don't feel much of anything at all, except perhaps anticipation around how events will unfold from now on. How will COBRA respond to it? How will Jay and Saz react? Will anyone be sorry, up sticks and call it a day? What will it mean for their fortunes? And for mine? I remember reading an account of four South African war photographers who'd gotten so caught up in trying to get just the right shot with just the right amount of light that they grew oblivious to the suffering they were there to witness.[3] One of the four, Joao Silva, wrote candidly of how the first thing he did when his friend and fellow photographer Ken Oosterbroek was shot and killed was to take pictures of him dead. Thinking about this afterwards, he blamed it on being 'in the zone', on doing what he knew best, and yet continued to feel haunted by his reaction. His other photographer-friend, Kevin Carter, ended up taking home the Pulitzer Prize for his image of a Sudanese girl being stalked by a vulture. Published in *Life Magazine*, his photo took the world by storm: everyone wanted to know what he did to help the girl. It wasn't until the evening of the prize ceremony at Columbia University that Carter came clean to his editor. He told her he hadn't done anything at all – rather, he had spent twenty minutes working the scene, hoping that the vulture would spread its wings to make for a more arresting photograph.

How is it that we appear to have no empathy when it should matter most?

It doesn't take long for responses to the suicide to show up in our team chatroom. Lindsey asks us to refer to her from now on as 'Casper' (the ghost) instead. Two other hunters post emojis of a dancing girl, saying the man was a monster and so who gives a fuck.

'You okay, Saz?' I write.

'Not really jack between us as I want to hunt no more Xx. I feel shit someone killed themselves, although I know he done wrong but now his family are left behind because of me. I'm scared if the next one I stand in front of does the same and I feel like I have blood on my hands.'

We tell each other that we did warn the police that he threatened to end it all during the live streaming and that this should be on their body cams so the responsibility is really theirs.

'I have been grounding myself over the last 48 hours gardening (I know that's strange) and thinking the same thing. My only conclusion is he had the means to do this easy and painless and possibly been thinking of doing this previously and I put the cherry on the cake, so to speak. I'm still having nightmares so I'm going to have to face this and go on the next strike and see if this helps or walk away. No problem we will send the chat logs as we trust you and please destroy when you are finished with them. Xx'

A few days later, on a rare visit, I explain my fieldwork to my parents. They tell me something I never knew about my family. I tell Saz. She writes back straightaway:

> Oh! Jack I held my breath through reading that but the freedom you have just given your family, is more than words can say. This is what its about jack people breaking the silence and lifting the cloud over them, just a little bit. Heartbreakingly true back in those days they was never educated and possibly never understood at the time what was going on, as sex was a tabbo subjects. It kills ya inside doesn't it? You want your family to speak freely but wishing you never knew, all in one. Massive bear hugs and I'm sure your head is all over the place. You will always have a place with COBRA now and after your case. Next strike will we do in honor of your dear family. Xx

15

Made it just in time for tonight's sting in West London after a long day of teaching and heavy traffic. Unlike any of my prior stings, I haven't any information on who our target is and soon find out that I'm not the only one not in the know. There are far more of us here tonight than usual and faces I don't recognise.

The target is a doorman, Jay tells us, and 'a big fella', which is why he called on another team for help in case he tries to fight his way out of the confrontation. The team look the part: its leader is enormous and covered head-to-toe in tattoos, and the rest of them are scarcely less intimidating. Still, Jay seems uncertain, oscillating between advice from our guests and from whoever is on the other end of his phone. After fifteen minutes of this, we find out why. It seems that our predator is out drinking with his pals and neither he nor our guests have the appetite for exposing a doorman surrounded by friends who, as Jay says, will be shit-faced by the time we get to them. Everything about this sting spells trouble, says Jay, and so why don't we look at other options.

I take advantage of this breather to catch up with Steve, the new head of security at COBRA. I ask him how he got involved with COBRA. He tells me it all began when a sting popped up on his Facebook page:

> That brought back a lot of memories because the guy they stung was just so in denial and somebody mentioned, you know, the effects that this could have on children for the rest

of their lives, and I thought to myself, that's right; these people seem to think that because they're behind a computer screen, it's all okay, as if there's nobody else there, or that whatever is there isn't real. And so then I thought, yes I'd like to get into this, because even if only one child in a million can be saved this way then I've done something more than watching a video and pressed the 'like' button.

But then I thought, what if I was to come up against somebody that maybe knew me as a young boy, how would that make me feel? And I thought about this for a while and decided I'd be okay with that, and that's when I contacted Saz and Jay.

My first sting with them was of a guy who drove up to meet a child in a car park. We spotted him driving in and out of the car park and then back in again and parking right in the middle of it. And so one of us blocked the exit with their car while Jay and I walked up to him. When he saw us, he started his engine and drove straight at us and we jumped out of the way as he drove out of the car park through the entrance. But because Jay had his phone number, we called him and told him that we weren't going to harm him but did want to talk to him. Jay said we didn't really want to go to his house, and we didn't want to go to the university where he worked – and Jay told him exactly where he worked – and so then the predator said, Okay, what have I got to do?

And you know what, when we met up with him, he wasn't at all what I thought a predator looked like. He didn't look like the dirty old man with a raincoat and a brown paper bag stuffed with pornographic stuff, you know. And so then it hit me. He was like my teacher because, like my teacher he just looked so ordinary. And that brought home a lot of what happened to me, about how people lurk behind a façade of decency to commit the most horrible crimes.

I know there are people who disagree with what we do because they say What if predators go and kill themselves? But we don't go out on flimsy evidence. We've done our homework. Also, and it might be a nasty thing to say, but for me it's no great loss if they do. Because they are somebody's brother and son it's going to be hard for them to believe that they were an online predator, and once they've taken their own lives, there isn't going to be a trial in court where that family will see the evidence of him talking to children or having pictures of children on his devices, and until their family actually see that rock-solid evidence, it's going to be really difficult for them to believe their son or brother was a child molester.

My second sting left me worst affected. It was late in the evening, and we managed to get the predator out of his house, and he kept looking at me. He just kept looking at me and I nearly broke down because I felt that he knew that I was a victim. And what made all of it worse was that he was chatting to young boys as well. I felt that he knew about my abuse. And even now I still find it hard to look predators in the eyes because what if they know.

And then when you talk to predators, they often given the excuse of saying they were bored or lonely, and that they've never done anything like it before; that it was their first time. And, of course, people get bored and lonely, but their first choice shouldn't be to start grooming children. When you're bored you pick up a book or go for a walk. I can't see how or why being bored and lonely makes you want to hunt down a child. Like the last one we did, he asked a young girl whether she shaved herself, you know, and whether she'd had her period, and then started talking about what he wanted his dog to do to her. And you say you do that because you're bored? That makes no sense. Why not use adult sites? There are women out there that are bored or lonely and only want to meet somebody for one night. Why not do that instead?

We set off. Without offering any further details, Jay gives us a postcode to type into our GPS and tells us to park inconspicuously and stay out of sight of our target house. It's only a fifteen-minute drive from where we are, he says, and we want to make sure they don't get wind of our presence while we regroup. I am one of the first to arrive on the scene. By the time the others get there, Jay tells us that he did a 'walk by' and noticed four cars in the driveway. It means there could be as many as eight adults inside, Jay says, and so things could get a little hairy.

As we wait around the corner from the house, Jay and the other team's leader approach the house. Our target opens the door and, after brief introductions, obediently follows the team into a paved area between the cars and his garage. It is getting dark, and Steve turns on the light on his smartphone. Saz starts the live stream as soon as our suspect has confirmed that the photograph sent to our decoy child is his. So far, the sting's much like any other.

As the suspect begins to talk, he does not seem to realise that we are live streaming the conversation. Perhaps it is because of Steve's smartphone light, obscuring his view of us, or perhaps he hasn't caught on to the implications of being exposed, for why else would he tell us from the get-go that his life is a shambles; that he is stuck in a loveless marriage; that he hasn't had sex for months; that his son has Downs and his wife wants to give the child up for adoption; that he is so bored with life?

Jay tries to stop him:

'Sir, there's no need,' he says, but our predator doesn't get it. So Jay tries again saying, 'We don't need to know any of this,' and points to the camera phone. 'All we want to know is why was you going for children online.'

It begins to rain. Our predator has on nothing more than pyjama trousers, a t-shirt and socks and, before long, is visibly shivering from the cold. His wife and two children meanwhile have gathered in the doorway. His daughter doesn't look older than 10 with the boy probably around 4 or so and keen to join his dad outside. His mum holds him back, saying that his dad will be coming in soon. The boy calls out to his dad, wondering aloud why he isn't responding. I'm finding it hard to watch and retreat from the mob to do the usual: to call the police to make the arrest and put a stop to all this.

The police are caught up in the aftermath of a protest elsewhere in London and can give us no definitive time frame. Saz hands me the camera phone – she needs a smoke she says – and the predator and I make eye contact for the first time. What might he be thinking, I wonder. I have an overwhelming sense that he's asking me to help him but how can I? What would help look like other than what I've already done to get the police on the scene as soon as possible? And so I stare back at him in return, worrying that doing anything else but toughen up would give away how compromised I really feel. For all I know, he may have already seen through the damn charade.

The interrogation is relentless but not without merit. He admits to grooming at least another two children online, one of who is a 'pre-teen', and that admission alone validates one of the reasons hunters continue to live stream stings: it allows decoys from other teams to recognise a predator and notify the sting team in real time that he's been grooming them too.

It seems that even among predators there is a hierarchy of sorts. Leaving aside those who have physically abused real children – most often within their own families or friendship circle – of those who confine their abuse to the online world, the 'pre-teen lot' are backwash to an already sordid genetic mutation. When Jay asks him 'why go for a pre-teen?' he's stumped for an answer. He says he doesn't know, and I wouldn't be surprised if he really doesn't.

There's fallout from this sting the morning after:

JAY HUNTER
Just had the officer for last nights sting asking me to take down the video to avoid charges against us

STEVE HUNTER
That is absolutely disgusting from that officer

JAY HUNTER
Just had a bit of a heated chat with her when he admitted he's a predator I get assaulted an nothing is done about it

STEVE HUNTER
FFS you should say you wanna press charges against his sisters for assault. The sisters are poisonous dwarfs x

SAZ DECOY
The officer was fine when I spoke to her yesterday but today she really isn't happy lol xx

JAY HUNTER
Yep totally different person today. Good thing is they only have mine and Saz's details on this sting

STEVE HUNTER
that's ok then

What Saz and Jay thought might blow over didn't. Two months later, I receive a call from the police, asking me to please provide them with a witness statement following legal charges filed by the predator against COBRA. I haven't any desire to testify against Saz and Jay, and nor do I think it helpful. The officer tells me I've not yet been subpoenaed and whether or not I choose to contribute at this point is entirely my choice. I tell her about my ongoing fieldwork and explain how it has been helping the police. I am not at all sure that my testimony will advance the predator's case beyond what's already available in the sting video on Facebook, but am fairly certain that testifying against COBRA will mean losing access to the field. Perhaps unfairly, I ask her whether she thinks that it's a price worth paying? She tells me she understands and that's the last I hear of it.

Weighing up the cost of giving testimony against an uncertain (and perhaps slim) benefit was probably the right thing to do. And yet I can't help but feel like I let a vulnerable someone down. I remember how, years ago, I read Joe Badaracco's *Defining Moments*, in which he explains that many decisions we face aren't of the 'right vs wrong' kind but 'right vs right', in that both can be justified, even if both involve compromise – either in terms of our personal values or, in Badaracco's specific case, a business opportunity. This feels kind of like one of those. If it is, what then does it say about me?

16

I wake up to a breaking news story by an independent television channel. It is 13 August 2020.

> The Vice Principal at one of the UK's most prestigious ballet schools has resigned after an ITV News investigation revealed allegations he had been grooming his teenage students for sex.
>
> Jonathan Barton, who worked at Ballet West Scotland in Argyll, has been accused of abusing his position to sleep with 16-year-old pupils at the £9,000 a year boarding school his family runs in Taynuilt.
>
> Our investigation has heard from more than sixty women – former students, staff and parents – who have given us their accounts of the Ballet West teacher's inappropriate behaviour going back as far as 2004 and as recently as 2018.
>
> Jonathan Barton refutes all the claims made.

Ballet West's governing board made the decision to close the school with immediate effect. In an email to parents it said, among other things:

> As soon as we were made aware of the ITN allegations, the Board decided to suspend the Vice Principal. He offered his resignation immediately, and it was accepted on August 11.
>
> Following the broadcast of an allegation against the Principal, she was suspended on Friday August 14.

As a Board, we endeavoured to investigate the allegations regarding the Vice Principal and Principal, who is suspended from her post, as fully as possible in the short time available and we have told Police Scotland that we will make all possible information available to them.

Many parents have, rightly, expressed their outrage that anything improper could happen at the school. We are deeply sorry that so many of you have been put in such a distressing situation by events at Ballet West. Most importantly, we would like to offer an unreserved apology to students past and present and particularly those who feel the school failed to protect them.

My daughter asks if I can come up to Ballet West to collect her and take her home.[1]

17

Tonight's sting should be interesting Jay says as he lifts his paedo-pack out of the boot of his hatchback in the parking lot of a country pub in Northamptonshire. The pub and the few houses alongside it are surrounded by nothing but farmland as far as the eye can see. It is a stunningly beautiful afternoon.

I am first to arrive on the scene with our decoy Lindsey a close second. Saz writes to say that they're running late, having made a pitstop at a KFC. Apparently, it took all of thirty minutes for Jay's chicken to arrive, after which they'd stopped at a Burger King because one of the others had wanted a burger instead. She says that I might run into a couple of lads from Leeds who are only just around the corner and will arrive before they do. They should be easy to spot, she says.

As Lindsey lights up she tells me what a horrible beast today's predator is and how hard the decoying had been on her psychologically. He'd created an online profile, she says, where he called himself BigBlackJohn and used a photo catfished online of a black man. They did a Google reverse image search of the photo but that didn't turn up anything useful, she says, and they didn't find out until late in the conversation that he isn't black at all but white, and in his 70s.

Lindsey tells me that he began talking to two other COBRA decoys believing they were young sisters and brazenly asked these 'girls' for a phone number for their mum. It's a rare move on his part and so rare in fact that COBRA have only ever seen one other example like it. The decoy-girls give him their mum's number, the decoy-mum being Lindsey. She pulls out her phone and shows me screenshots of what he'd asked her to do for him:

BIGBLACKJOHN

I'm John into property investment 40 yrs old been married 2 kids boy+girl don't live with me. Now i'm into meeting mothers with young daughters for sex, your youngest is to young but will fuck you and your 13 and 15hr old daughters if you want me to, I don't use condoms so what you say

LINDSEY DECOY

So what is your companys name then May be looking for some property

BIGBLACKJOHN

I don't sell property, just rent out houses

LINDSEY DECOY

Ahh ok x what's the youngest girl you had sex with?

BIGBLACKJOHN

the youngest was in india she said she was 17 but found out she was really just 15 yrs old but it was real good with her

LINDSEY DECOY

wow ok how many you had sex with

BIGBLACKJOHN

A few why, see you got a 15yr old what's her name, may-be you'd like me to add her to my conquests if you think she could handle me lol

LINDSEY DECOY

give me your phone number and will discuss this xx

BIGBLACKJOHN

don't give my number till I really know someone been storked after giving it out before had to change my number which was not easy with all my contacts

'How did you catch him?' I ask.

Lindsey says that one of the 'sisters' had done such a good job in grooming BigBlackJohn that he'd fallen head over heels for her and was desperate to meet face to face, with or without her mum. The problem was, she says, that he's white and the guy in his profile photo black, and so she wouldn't have known how to pick him out from a crowd were they to meet in a public space. So she asked him to send her a recent photo of himself so she'd know who to look out for, and to be sure it's really him, to show himself touching his nose with his right hand.

Hard to believe, Lindsey says, but he did as asked, and seeing how the shot was taken with his camera phone, Jay was able to access the metadata and get access to GPS coordinates of where the photo had been taken. These coordinates identified a house on the opposite side of the road from our car park, almost entirely hidden from view by trees.

'Just goes to show how we decoys groom the guys who think they are grooming us,' Lindsey says, though she also tells me that she feels guilty about grooming predators that way.

'But I don't feel bad for this guy,' she says, 'cause he's the worst I've seen.'

A white VW Polo pulls into the parking lot. Inside it are two of the biggest guys I've seen in my life, alongside a third, in the backseat, who is only fractionally smaller. Their 'uniform' shows them to be from a different hunting team, called here by Jay to help out on what could be a troublesome sting. There's a pub opposite the house and if people from the pub decide to intervene it could mean trouble all round.

'Thank fuck that's a German ride,' Lindsey says as they pull up, 'or the front axle wouldn't have survived.'

'Can't run,' Jay later says, 'but can stop of a truck dead.' I know what he means.

The big boys look at me sideways until Saz tells them that I am 'a good 'un'; that I was with them and I'm 'alright'. It's all they need to know.

Lindsey and I use the pub's facilities and leave 50 pence on the bar in lieu of buying drinks. We rejoin Jay, Saz, Steve, Winston and the boys to take our final instructions. Jay and Steve will knock on the door with the rest of us following behind to keep an eye out for anyone leaving the pub. The trees obscuring the house from view will prove a blessing in disguise. Saz will do the live streaming. He has a portable power bank at the ready, he says, in case she runs short. It's my job to call the police in due course.

Our target looks surprised at nine strangers on his front lawn. In a few words, Jay tells him who we are and why we're here. Winston meanwhile positions himself near enough to the open door to prevent him from going back inside and closing up on us. After all, there's every chance he will try to destroy whatever implicating material now sits on his devices.

I hold off on calling the police until Saz and Jay have had a few minutes with the predator, which is how they like it.

It isn't long before the predator's wife pokes her head around the corner to ask what's going on. 'Why don't we go and talk inside, and I'll tell you why we're here,' Lindsey says. The wife looks uncertain but invites her into their living room. A window offers a view of the unfolding scene inside.

The interrogation proceeds much like they usually do: the predator denies all. Then, when confronted with the evidence, he admits that he carried on sexual chat but never once believed the decoys to be real children; that the 'daughter' he had wanted to meet wasn't a girl at all, no matter how old she said she was, but just another adult playing games online. They were having a laugh, he says.

Lindsey, meanwhile, has had her fill of him, having now also spoken to his wife. She steps outside and has a go at the predator. Your wife, she tells him, wants to kill you here and now, and then she begins to cry. Surprised at her own reaction, she walks off into the garden, and with nothing else to offer, I step forward and give her a hug.

Before the police arrive on the scene, his adult daughter does, after a call from her mother. She immediately presses Jay for details, wanting to know what her father had said and done online and to whom, before joining her mum in the living room. Through the window, I can see her rocking her mother in her arms. Their pain will be from a place so deep that it embarrasses me to be looking on. These poor people must be having the worst day of their lives, I think, and here I am, a voyeur, with no obligation to respond to their vulnerability.

Jay, Steve and the big boys are becoming agitated, or maybe excited, and as I move closer, I discover why. In talking to the predator's daughter, they found out that she's a prison officer and, as if that isn't enough of a coincidence, she works the 'nonce's wing'.

She could get into serious trouble if any of the prisoners were to find out what her own father's been up to.

'You couldn't make this stuff up if you tried,' Jay says later.

BigBlackJohn hasn't any intention to roll with the blows and on being arrested tries to persuade the police to force COBRA to take the uploaded footage down from Facebook. Saz and Jay have no such intention.

But, the next morning, the sting video is gone from COBRA's Facebook page. Jay re-uploads it, adding an explanation:

> this video keeps going down the multi millionair who cat fished another mans profile grooming a mother and 2 daughters for sex also 2 other 12 yr olds ame forward get this mans face out there

When the re-uploaded video is again taken down by Facebook, the team posts it once more, this time accompanied by four screenshots featuring the predator. Convinced that our predator's lawyer is behind the 'vandalism', they address him directly in a new post:

> Just in case Catfish-Grandpa is watching, thank you for smiling for the camera. Keep reporting and the more copies go up. If someone puts out a post asking for everyone to reupload it in your local area, they will. Then you will have fifty, a hundred, goodness knows how many. You are best off just leaving it up here and accepting that you got caught. Change yourself, not the evidence of what you are.

It isn't hard to understand their rage towards predators like him who ask mothers to facilitate sex with their daughters, and then try to duck the bullet. Yet to me it feels important to be able to differentiate between levels of severity of harm inflicted and whether this harm was inflicted on a real child or a decoy. There are some, like Catfish-Grandpa, who seek to meet a real child and come prepared for the occasion. Others get their kicks from talking sexually to a child, whether real or pretend. Then there are exhibitionists who enjoy the thought of children watching them engage in a sexual act even if they have no desire to physically seek them out, and those who may well have pulled out of a sexual conversation had it not been for the active grooming by a decoy. Don't get me wrong: all these acts are nefarious and also illegal, or at least in the UK they are, but the point is that they are nefarious in degrees.

Over the next few weeks and then months, I come to understand how significantly stings impact predators' family members who often had no idea what their spouse, partner, son or father was up to online. The first indication of it comes in a letter sent by the wife of a predator stung by Saz and Jay's team.

On Sunday 20th January 2019, at around mid-day, I was in bed recovering from an invasive procedure 4 days before to obtain several biopsies confirming I had Cancer. As anyone can imagine mentally I was in a very dark place and physically very weak.

I heard the front door being knocked, living in a bungalow my bedroom was only about 15' from the front door. My husband answered the door and I heard a male voice use his first name. My husband stepped outside and closed the door, I imagined it was a neighbour asking after my health and my husband not wishing to disturb me had stepped outside. I later learned this was not the case, he was ordered to step outside even though he protested that his wife was inside unwell and in bed.

After some time had passed and my husband had not returned indoors I got out of bed and through the frosted glass panel at the side of the front door I could see someone speaking to him. A voice I didn't recognise. I returned to bed.

More time passed and I was becoming increasingly concerned as to why my husband was still in conversation outside, clad only in trousers and a Tee shirt on a very cold damp day, and hadn't invited in whoever was outside.

Again, I got out of bed and heard a male voice loudly use the word 'Masturbation'. On hearing this word I opened the door where I was confronted by 6 or 8 individuals dressed in what appeared to be mainly black clothing with the words COBRA on their sleeves. In that split second moment for me COBRA meant something to do with civil emergencies or some such body allied to the government, what on earth could they be doing in my front garden talking to my husband? Was it to do with terrorism? They could have been armed for all I knew. The large male immediately to my right when I opened the door ordered me in a very intimidating and aggressive manner to get back inside my home.

In my weakened and vulnerable state emotionally and physically and dressed only in my nightdress and dressing gown, I began to shake uncontrollably and was on the verge of passing out with fright. I was absolutely terrified of what was happening. At no point did these individuals identify themselves, and thinking they were a team of professionals from the Police Force I complied and with the help of two women in the group whom I assumed to be detectives, I was assisted into my sitting room where I collapsed onto a sofa in great distress crying and shaking violently. I told them the reason I had been in bed, the one woman informing me her sister had recovered from Cancer. As if that made me feel any better in the circumstances I found myself in.

These two women then told me briefly the reason for their visit. They had a large file on my husband that in their words I wouldn't want to read!!!! They would not allow me to see or speak to my husband. I insisted he was given a coat as he is a 74 year old insulin dependent diabetic with multiple health issues including recovering from a fractured vertebrae. I was terrified he would have a heart attack.

I was desperately in need of help with the situation I found myself in, but I was not allowed to phone my daughter until the 2 women said I could. Because of the nature of their very intimidating presence and the manner in which I was ordered about and not allowed access to my husband or daughter I assumed they were a legal lawful force. By omission of identity at that stage I couldn't assume otherwise.

Horrifyingly I was told that the interview with my husband who would be named was being filmed at that very moment and being posted on certain websites on the Internet. I was totally traumatised by this, sobbing uncontrollably and unable stand up from the shock. The cruelty of this information, the way it was delivered and the future shame and degradation that would be directed at me in the fallout from it was unbearable. With hindsight the Police would not have been posting the situation on the Internet, but I was too upset to have rational thought as it all happened so quickly. What has happened to Innocent until proven Guilty? Why identify me by identifying him?

Eventually they said they had contacted the local police force who would now come and arrest my husband who would be taken into custody. (Their description of the uniformed police officers who would arrive is unprintable.) Only then was I allowed to phone my daughter which I did, after getting as far as telling my daughter there was a problem as a group of people in black were holding her father outside, the phone was taken from me and one of the women spoke to my daughter, my daughter arrived in about 30 minutes.

At no time did these individuals ask for permission to enter or be on my gated property, or permission to film thereon. When I was ordered back inside I only complied as I believed them to be a legal force, they didn't identify themselves and even said they didn't use their real names, which on reflection would have been very odd for the Police to say that, but at the time I just didn't take that fact in.

At this point in time I have had major abdominal surgery for Cancer followed by further treatment in the form of Radiotherapy, and who knows what my future is. The pressures of the last few months are not hard for anyone to imagine, trying to cope with the Cancer diagnosis, massive surgery, Radiotherapy, etc., the disintegration of my marriage, and the immense invasion of my privacy.

I am suffering from Post Traumatic Stress manifesting itself in appalling flashbacks to what happened to me that day, insomnia, medication for depression, I am unable to answer the telephone or front door, and visions of those awful, vile uninvited individuals in my front garden, and the strangers who came into my home where I very much felt I was a hostage. I am wrecked mentally, my future hopes have disappeared and at times I am suicidal, for which I am now receiving medical help. I was left feeling completely humiliated by them and unable to stand up for myself in any way. Unlike the Police they obviously do not consider they have any Duty of Care towards the wider families. What if we had visiting relatives, grandchildren or friends with us at the time, they would have been traumatised too.

I am totally uninvolved with whatever my husband was held and interviewed and filmed about. As a law abiding 70 year old woman living a quiet life in a small cul-de-sac in a tiny rural community, no thought was given to me and the fact that my near neighbours would see and hear all, and whatever verdict comes later the implications for me will stick. I am an innocent victim who was traumatised beyond belief in her own home by the behaviour of these thoroughly unwholesome individuals masquerading as some legal force, who in all honesty on reflection looked like a ridiculous but sinister S.W.A.T. team of vigilantes from an American T.V. series.

Along with my serious health issues, and the state of my marriage, my life now and in the future is in pieces, their behaviour being a huge contributary factor in my inability to cope. How can this be allowed to happen in this manner here in the United Kingdom, where innocent citizens such as myself can be irreparably damaged for life in this way.

Do I not have any Human Rights or Right of Privacy in law? Should they be allowed to enter a gated property and home without any permission from the owners and film thereon? Surely something can be done to ensure these aggressive 'Gangs' of Vigilantes, an apt description of them can be stopped from masquerading as a legal arm of the law.

Importantly, for the invasion of my privacy, distress, trauma, harassment, and removal of my freedoms in my own home and on my property, especially in the fragile state of health I was and continue to be in, they deserve to be arrested and cautioned for their behaviour that day and maybe even charged under a law that must exist somewhere, relating to their treatment of me on that occasion, if only to protect in future any other vulnerable adults, families and children who may be innocently caught up their seriously harmful behaviour and affected in the short or long term.

I write to her and ask to speak by phone. I'd like her to provide me with a bit more context. We speak a few days later. She tells me while Jay and Vince took her husband outside for questioning after a 'doorknock', Saz asked her if she could be allowed to come inside for a chat to explain what was going on. At first, she says, I thought they were law enforcement. Especially after Saz told me she had evidence that implicated my husband in a terrible crime. The problem was that she wouldn't show any of it to me but what she said made me so uncomfortable that I ended up putting my head on her shoulders and cried. What she feels so bitter about, she tells me, is that she was taken for a fool, thinking these were good people while they weren't. Her husband was then arrested, and their computers confiscated and, she says, 'I still haven't heard anything back and nor have any formal charges been brought.' Had he been caught red-handed while trying to meet a child, it would have made a world of difference, she tells me. For one, her house wouldn't have been soiled by the experience of hunters entering it. As it is, she no longer feels safe in her own home. What makes it all the more galling is that her husband knew that she herself was abused by her mum's partner when she was only 12 years old, leaving her wondering why he'd done something horrible like this. Even so, for hunters to come to their house that day to expose her husband in such a public way was, for her, the bigger offence. She tells me she is still receiving EMDR treatment to help her cope with the impact even if the sting took place over a year ago. She then says she'll ask her daughter to provide her account of the experience too.

The next day I receive an email from her daughter describing her experience of the sting:

> I received a phone call from my mother saying that there were people at the house from COBRA because my father had done something and that lots of people were at the house, two inside and lots outside. She needed me to go over there. It was all really confused and garbled as she was in a very vulnerable state, in the end a woman came on to the telephone. She took control of the conversation. This woman told me she couldn't give me her name but my father was being filmed live because he had been caught online grooming. I asked if was for TV, she said it for being filmed online. She said she wasn't sure how

they could stop the video but she realised that they needed support for my mother. I asked if they were the police and she said that the police were on their way. They needed me there because of my mother, they didn't expect someone to be at the property, except for me.

As I arrived there were two men at the gate way, three men and a woman with dad outside the front door. They looked menacing. The two men at the gate discussed something and one walked over. The man came over to me and asked me who I was and if I was the daughter. I asked him for identification first before we discussed anything further. He looked confused. Another man came over. Both of them very intimidating, blocking me from entering my property. I asked him for his identification. He said he didn't have any and that he didn't need any. He told me that COBRA is a charity. I told him I had already looked up the group and that I couldn't find anything on them and so I wasn't entirely sure they were a charity. I said you need identification as a charity or as someone going to people's houses. He gave me some information about why they were there, without me asking for it, and he said that they were waiting for the police. I said they were on my private property and didn't have permission to be on there. I stated that I did not give them permission to film me, my father or my property. He said they did have the right to be there. I asked for evidence and he said 'you won't want to see it.' I told him not to tell me what I do and do not want.

When I got to my father, the woman filming lowered her camera. The three men there blocked me, the two from the road came behind me and I had no choice but to go through the front door. I asked to speak to the person in charge or spokesperson. They said there wasn't a spokesperson. They said I needed to go into the house because otherwise I would end up on camera and that it would affect my job as I'm a teacher. One man said that I should call the police on them if I wasn't happy with them being there.

I was greeted by a woman who also couldn't give me identification. She told me she could only give me a fake name. Another woman was sitting on the sofa opposite my mother. I went past the woman in the hallway into the lounge where my mother was sitting on the sofa. She told me that the ladies had been really kind to her. In essence, they had trapped her in the lounge and wouldn't let her out of the front door. She was very upset and knew she was trapped but couldn't do anything about it. The ladies were walking around the main part of the house like they lived here. We were trapped because there were two in the house and three by the front door. Two at the gate. The lady filming was making it difficult because I didn't want to appear on camera, and she used this as a form of deterrent so you couldn't use the front door.

I demanded to see the file of evidence. She gave me an envelope. She told me that I would see photographs of my father naked.

I told the ladies they needed to leave and said I wanted my father back inside. I asked if they were trained in dealing with the situation of a family in like this scenario and she said they don't need to be trained in anything. They are a charity who help children. I said again I had tried to find them on Google and nothing came up, and that it is illegal to portray yourself as a charity if you are not a charity. She had no answer. She said my best option if I wasn't happy was to call the police on them.

I told the man and the woman that I wasn't happy about: the lack of identification; their lack of ability to deal with family members; what if there had been children in the house; that they give fake first names and won't give whole name; that they intimidating to family members; that they don't come up on any search engine to check their validity of who they say they are; that they state they are a charity and I couldn't find them online; that the video was live and uploaded straight away; that they refused to leave my property when asked; that the two women had trapped my mother and come across to her as kind but that I wasn't happy with the way they had treated her or the information they had given her and that they had made the home unsafe for her; that the lady in the kitchen had tried to touch me and comfort me when it was obvious I didn't need that; that they are clueless in how to deal with people; that their language was inappropriate.

I said that obviously this is a highly emotional situation but that I was still unhappy with the way they had dealt with my mother and how do I make a complaint? They said I had to go to the police but it would affect my father's case if I made a complaint and that they would share the video.

Later, I receive an email from someone at the Home Office wondering if I'd be interested in hearing accounts of family members of other predators and, if so, if I'd be happy for her to pass on my contact details so they could speak directly with me. I tell her I'd be happy to hear from any family members and, before long, receive another two emails. Neither involve COBRA. But they are insightful enough to warrant republishing in full.

The day started out as pretty normal. I did a bit of shopping and then went back home to clean up. The afternoon school run completed it was time to go home and start on a child's costume for school the next day. We all did it together as a family. Little did we know he wouldn't be wearing it the next day.

At around 6.30pm my partner jumped up from the sofa, went to the kitchen and paced around for about three minutes. I followed him through to see what was concerning him so much he had to pace. He told me there was a police officer on the phone who told him they had arrested someone for using his identity. There were four more phone calls after that, all from a withheld number. I answered the calls and was given a name of the police officer, PC Anderson, along with a crime reference number. They said they were sending local police over to take a statement.

Something about these calls didn't sit well with me and so I contacted the police force this person had said he was from. I was told that there was no crime reference number and no police officer of that name within the force.

So, I went ahead and contacted our local police force and logged it as an incident just to be on the safe side. They advised me to keep an eye on our bank accounts and not to open the door to anyone without an identity badge. In the knowledge that I was safe at home and that this incident had been reported to our local police force, I carried on finishing our child's costume. I hadn't eaten so decided to order a takeaway. My youngest and eldest had gone to bed. Two others were still awake.

At 10.50pm I decided I was going to bed. I told my partner and he said he was going to follow me up. At this point there was a knock on the door. It was loud and aggressive. Now usually I would have gone to the door but something stopped me. I went to the front room window instead, pulled the curtain across and saw two men. One tall and skinny dressed in dark clothing and the other short dressed in grey tracksuit bottoms and a blue bomber jacket. The tall one had a bodycam on the right side and a walkie talkie on the left side. He was also carrying a folder with what looked like scraps of paper inside.

After the phone call earlier, I thought they may be police and the 101 operator had made a mistake when checking the officers name. However, it soon became apparent that these were not police. They asked for my partners name and asked if he was home. They started screaming and shouting 'Where is he? Get him out now! He's a nonce.' I remember thinking out aloud and said 'woah hold on a minunte.' But they continued to scream in the street. At this point my legs buckled and I went into fight or flight mode. I couldn't process what was being said. I realised that both of the children who were still awake had come to stand by me. One was holding my pj top tightly, the other was stood there shaking like I had never seen before. It is a fear that I never want to see in any of my children's faces ever again. Even now, four months on, their faces from that night still haunt me.

One of them went and woke the eldest up, who staggered down the stairs not having a clue what was going on but could hear these men shouting and screaming the word 'nonce' almost like a chant in our front garden. We realised that there was another two men by the back gate who had balaclavas on also dressed in dark clothing.

I asked them for proof of what they were saying. The tall one just kept flicking his phone at me, not allowing me the time to read. My eldest daughter was screaming 'I want to see. My mums asking for the proof and you're not showing her.' They laughed at her and then laughed at all of us, telling us to send my partner out. My partner went to walk towards the front door to go out to them. My daughter slammed the front room door and refused him to go out she screamed 'please don't, there's loads with masks on.'

The middle daughter walked to the kitchen to get a drink and started to scream. I turned around to see a man with a balaclava trying to climb through my kitchen window. My daughters legs went from underneath her. I ran over and pushed him out with a bit of a struggle, pulling his mask halfway up his face to see the bottom half of his face and shut the window.

It was then that they started to push down on the door handles, both front and back door. The more the children objected to him going outside to them the more aggressive and intimidating they became, screaming and shouting louder.

I tried to dial 999 but as it was the end of the day my phone battery died as I tried dialling 999. My partner's phone had also lost its charge. The tall man then took his phone and dialled 999. He seemed aggressive on the phone to the emergency services operator. Whilst waiting for police to arrive, they continued to tell one my youngest that 'its ok, daddy won't hurt you again,' and 'we are here to protect you.'

Police arrived shortly later and removed them to the bottom of the street. They came into the house and the first officer could see that everyone in the house was visibly shaken, in shock and clearly traumatised. He turned to me and said 'we don't condone their behaviour one bit.' He told us that his sergeant was coming over to view their evidence and decide from there.

I couldn't function. I started to shake. My mouth was watering, and I knew the tell-tale signs of what was to come. I started to be sick. I was crying. I remember thinking 'what on earth just happened?'

Then came the news over the radio that they were arresting my partner. The local police officers handled everything so well. They wouldn't put the cuffs on my partner so as not to cause more distress to the children. My partner told me that he had been on a 18+ dating app called 'sweet meet' but he genuinely didn't know or believe he had been speaking to a child. They asked about devices. They took my laptop, his phone and the PS4 in our bedroom.

With the door locked, it was me and my four children. I sat looking around at the children and realised the complete and utter devastation this had and was going to have on me and them. I cried, I broke, I hugged my children tighter that night than I've probably ever hugged them knowing this was the start. I knew what these groups entailed. I had sat and watched them making judgements on the people they caught. Now this was my life. My children's lives.

Within half an hour, my daughters and I started to receive screenshots from the hunters' social media page. They became extremely upset because this was their stepdad; someone who had been in their lives for 11 years; who had showed them right from wrong; who had protected them; who had worked all the hours to provide for them.

They all finally fell asleep at 6am. I had already made the conscious decision to not send them to school the next day and sat there for the rest of the night into the next morning watching people we knew, close friends, people we had helped when they themselves were struggling or being judged by people in the community posting comments online. My heart broke into 1000 pieces.

The custody sergeant rang me the following day to say they were releasing my partner under investigation and without conditions. They told him to go live his life as a free man. They would contact him in due course should they need to. I repeated what the hunters had told me. He explained to me not to listen to everything they had told me and to take it all with a pinch of salt.

Social services turned up late the day after and didn't even ask how any of us were doing. They made me sign a safety plan to state that partner was not allowed back in the property and then left.

The hunter continued to ring for a week after in the early hours of the morning to tell me various bits of the supposed conversations my partner had had online. He also rang friends of mine that had commented on their social media post and told them what had been supposedly said in conversations. He rang my partner's workplace and told them. They immediately dismissed him so as not to bring the company's name into disrepute. I was told my children would be removed as the hunter's mum was head of the local social services. I quote 'in a click of my fingers, I will have them removed.' He told me he had given his phone number to my neighbours, and they would ring him should my partner be seen anywhere near my house.

I rang the schools to inform them of what had happened and explained the children when they returned would need help. My mental health took a nosedive. I wasn't eating. I wasn't sleeping. I couldn't breathe. My chest felt like someone was sitting on it constantly. My eyes were sore. I didn't wash. I didn't brush my teeth. I took the youngest to school and would go home and sit gazing at the walls. TV would be on but just as background noise. My eldest daughter took care of cooking food.

I knew I wasn't thinking rationally, I knew I needed help. I was struggling, I was having suicidal thoughts and it didn't just concern me. The thoughts were to take me and my children away from the complete devastation we called life. To take them from the rumours that followed that night, the looks of pity, the looks of disgust, the sly and disgust looks, the comments mainly by fully grown adults, the giggling in school corridors.

I contacted a mental health crisis service. I cried all the way there. I cried in the waiting room. I completely broke when I went into to see the nurse. I told them about the thoughts, about how I was trying so hard to control them thoughts. About how my rationale was being just the protective factor for my children and removing us all from the situation that at that time was just getting harder. Little did I know that this then would be used against me with social services.

The children continued to suffer. We had to tell our youngest that his dad was working away, although I think he cottoned on quite fast that there was something wrong. He struggled with regulating his emotions, sleeping at night in his own room and even now four months on continues to sleep in my bedroom alongside me. The two girls who saw and heard the most suffered immensely. They are frightened to be in their own home believing that these men will continue their campaign against us. We are now looking at relocating to a different area for a fresh start and have been given priority. This will mean moving the children's schools, for them also to make new friends.

Their education has been non-existent for four months. They still don't sleep properly, suffering nightmares. I hear them screaming in their sleep. I've gone in before now and one child is up the corner screaming and shaking still fast asleep.

Everything can be a trigger. For example, we've had a few hot days and I've accidently left the washing on the line, grey trousers hanging on the washing line in the dark. It's triggered her into an anxiety attack. Noises outside such as the wind banging the gate or a garden fence are triggers. Cars pulling up outside can affect them immensely. People passing by the house talking can send their minds into overdrive. Walking the street to or from school, they believe everyone is watching them, laughing at them, wanting to lash out at them. They've been screamed at in the street and recorded by children and most importantly fully grown adults. One of the girls suffered so much anxiety after the sting she started to soil herself through fear. It took them nearly two months for them to allow me to open the front room curtains. They put our dining room chairs under door handles so to stop anyone pulling the handles down. Then there is so much more.

The two that were in the room at the time have had to start counselling both inside and outside school. They have intervention on the days they do actually go to school and are allowed to leave a class should they get overwhelmed. Schools have been brilliant and supportive. One child now self-harms due to overwhelming fear of being at home. She's 11 years old.

They all struggle with not seeing their dad/stepdad. It was just over a month before any contact was set up and to be perfectly honest I don't think social services wanted to grant even that. We had to travel over 60 miles to meet up so he could see his children. Even though it still was and is classed as an alleged offence it would have made their jobs a lot easier if I was to say I didn't want the kids to see him at all.

The social care system was and is shocking. I was never asked if I was ok or what support they could put in place for me or the children. I was left for weeks with no contact and when they were sent a report of my mental health assessment, they wanted to up the level of protection as they saw me as risk to the children. My childhood history of neglect was used against me, apparently making me incapable of making positive decisions for my own children.

We are five months in and continue to suffer on a daily basis. Intrusive thoughts, panic attacks and anxiety rule our lives.

After doing research on the group that attended our property, it seems all is not so well in the community of hunting. They argue amongst themselves like a pack of wild animals and it's hard to decipher which team is here for the better of children. The group that attended to our property are very well known for their own antics of drug dealings, stalking and harassing women, County lines, putting vulnerable women and children at risk by giving out address, livestreaming innocent men, including recently adding a veteran onto his hunting page and allowing followers to believe this man was a paedophile (that veteran very nearly took his own life). Both the lead hunter and team have numerous criminal convictions with the lead hunter still having open cases ongoing against him and have both served time at HMP for the above crimes.

I appreciate you giving me the opportunity to allow me to tell you my experience with these so-called hunters. I only hope telling my experience can make people see the lasting effects it has on innocent people and mainly innocent children.

I continue to receive evidence of the impact of stings on family members, including this one, from the sister of a suspect who killed himself after being exposed. He was only in his mid-thirties and father to a young girl.

I received a phone call from police to tell me that my brother had been arrested for child sex offences. There were photographs and conversations found on his phone that he was then being investigated for. He had been removed from the family home and was then on bail pending trial. As you will be aware, 2020 was Covid year and due to the backlog of cases and how they were having to deal with issues his case got waylaid for quite some time. He was actually due to go on trial for 3 days soon. He had a previous trial booked last year however due to the prosecution wanting a psych assessment, the case fell apart and a new date was set.

During this time, five people knew of his case, his ex-partner, myself and my husband and my uncle (who is five years older than me so effectively is like a big brother) and his wife. For three years, we kept him alive because no-one was aware of what was going on. Not even my parents.

I then received a phone call from my uncle who called to tell me that unfortunately John had been caught in a sting operation by an organisation called The Avengers. It was live streamed over Facebook whereby thousands, literally thousands had viewed this video, shared it, plastered him name everywhere and took a view as to his guilt. They had cornered him outside of his work, questioned him, interrogated him and spread his name and face for all to see all over social media.

Three weeks later, my mum had a visit from two police officers to inform her that John had taken his own life and was found in the caravan that he had been residing in having taken a highly toxic substance (we believe it was some kind of cyanide substance that he had ingested and would have been dead within 15–20 minutes). It was likely that he had been there for a couple of days.

The fall-out from his death has been absolutely catastrophic. Now, I want to make it clear that in no way whatsoever do I condone his actions, support his actions or understand his actions. We had been estranged since the first incident and hadn't spoken for the three years that his first case had been ongoing.

His death has left behind a 3-year-old daughter who, rightly or wrongly, will never ever get the opportunity to know her daddy. That option has been taken away from her. She will never know his voice. She will never get to see him again. He and his ex-partner had remained on relatively good terms and she had said that at some point in the future, had he received the right help, therapy, medication etc, there may have been a way for him to be in his daughter's life but this will now never happen. My parents and my elderly grandparents now have to attend the cremation of their son and grandson which should never have happened and it is all down to the actions of the organisation that collared him outside of his work and plastered him all over the internet.

No-one should be allowed to play judge, jury and executioner and that is exactly what happened. The police investigation from 2020 was dealt with in such a way that he stayed alive. Then, in three weeks these people have destroyed countless lives, and not just his. They do not think about the bigger picture, the family left behind, the fact that there could be a case of a mistaken identity (one of my friends had a similar case and the husband was plastered all over the internet but it was actually one of his work colleagues who had logged on as someone else and this person took his own life as no-one would believe him that he wasn't the one who had done it), mental disability, is the person going to get a fair trial now they have been put all over social media etc, his partner and child were at risk because these people had disclosed information about them, names, location etc. Since his death, we have since found out that it was extremely likely he was schizophrenic/bi-polar (which in no way makes him any less guilty) but does change the perspective of his mental health and wellbeing.

Something needs to be done whereby the act of live-streaming needs to be made illegal. These people are dangerous, taking the law into their own hands and not caring about the consequences of their actions.

We have to now find a way to navigate an innocent 3-year-old through her life without her daddy. At some point she will have to find out that his death was due to suicide and she will forever question why was she not enough to keep him alive. They do not care about this, but for those of use left behind, this is now something we will have to try and get out heads around and try and understand how utterly destroyed he was that he felt his only option was to take his own life.

My reaction to reading these is frustration with the punishment that is meted out so indiscriminately by hunters regardless of the severity of predators' crimes, and with little consideration for what, as far as I can see, are largely innocent bystanders – wives, siblings, children – who are often as abhorred by child grooming as hunters are.

But there are also those who remain deeply grateful to COBRA for having safeguarded their child and putting the predator behind bars. Here's a letter sent to me by a mother.

Finding inappropriate messages from a so-called friend on my 13-year-old daughter's phone led me to phone the police in the hope of them checking his devices. No nothing! The police reckon the predator hasn't said enough! My husband and I immediately started to contact Paedophile Hunter groups on social media. Children Online Battling Real Abuse (COBRA) agreed to help us. They set up a group call to discuss details and a group chat so we could share information to the hunters and decoys. One of the amazing decoys took over my daughter's chat.

After months of disgusting chat the team at COBRA went to confront the predator. Of course the narcissistic vile excuse of a man made a plea of not guilty a week later.

Communication with the court was sparse. Reserve dates for a trial came and went. Second reserve dates also passed. Finally, after almost 3 years from that first message to our daughter, 2 years from COBRA confronting him, we attended court. The trial was set for 3 days. Seven days of anxiety and stress, attending court each day, dealing with the predator's incompetent solicitor. She kept asking for more evidence, calling on more witnesses, like two whole years wasn't enough time to get this shit together!

The jury found him guilty of sexual communication with a child after only 50 minutes of deliberation. Fanbloodytastic. We were all so happy none of the jury believed the predator's lies.

Sentencing was set for a month later. No, didn't happen, yet another delay. Two months after the guilty verdict, we all travel hundreds of miles again to hear the judge serve the predator 20 months imprisonment. Silent cheers all round from us lot in the public gallery. Relief is an understatement for sure. Although that was only the start of what was to come. Anxiety and depression set in big time. Doctors, mental health nurse and counselling appointments came thick and fast for myself and our daughter. We had all stayed strong for so long, this was the 'come down' happening. COBRA were all still there for us. One of the team are always available for a message or a phone call. Helpful advice and words of wisdom because they know what we went through during and after. From the very first message and phone call, COBRA have been amazing. Full of knowledge and understanding, experience and compassion. Team COBRA supported us through our toughest times as a family, often checking up on our daughter. Supporting all of us before, during and after our awful court ordeal. Without team COBRA we would not have had a conviction and we certainly wouldn't be the same family as we are today. Stronger than ever!

I open Facebook Messenger to tap into the latest COBRA team chat. Much of it, as so often, is unrelated to hunting, even if helpful in understanding why hunters opt for such extreme methods to, as they put it, keep children safe.

SCOTT HUNTER
I'm meeting up with my parents (who I haven't spoke to for coming up 5 years) on Sunday. It could go 1 of 2 ways. All is well and we make a day of it Or I have to get out of there lively, meet you lot, you have to be my alibi, and I get an early inheritance. It's literally 50/50

SAM HUNTER
I've not spoken to my Mum in over 18 years and another 18 years suits me

SCOTT HUNTER
I'm the same mate. I'm literally no worse off for not having them in my life. One of my sisters has arranged it and said they 'need' talk to me. We'll see

SAM HUNTER
Well wish you well mate. Me and my sister both agreed if/ when she goes over we ain't going to no funeral. She put me through hell and scared me all my life

LINDSEY DECOY
If only we could choose our families I haven't spoken to my brother who I was so close to for 7 years I can't even look at his wife I Wana smash her face in is the Megan markle of our family a vial creature

SAM HUNTER
I've been advised many times to report the person who gave birth to me for the abuse I suffered at her hands

BILL HUNTER
Yup not seen my kids for 11yrs because of my ex wife. They are 20 and 17 now

SAM HUNTER
My mate in the same boat

LINDSEY DECOY
Oh don't get me started on the man who donated his sperm I don't care if he has cancer he is a disgusting spinless excuse of a man. He tried to run me over when I was 13 he watched my mum take an over dose and taunted her and never even

called an ambulance I was almost 12 I had to deal with her and my little brothers and sister I will never forgive him and when I was told he had prostate cancer I said good he deserves it. I don't give second chances but I let him into my children's lives for the very shortest time I told him this is Ur only chance blow it and it's game over. As predicted he did his usual trick. He can't keep his u know what in his pants and is hen pecked by his now wife who has fleeced him for every penny he has. And when he brags about his kids and grandkids I always make ppl know what I have today is my own making and the kind of woman I am is down to my mum he played zero part in my life

Ballet West's Jonathan Barton meanwhile has been charged with sixteen sexual offences, including four counts of rape. He made no plea at Oban Sheriff Court.

I'm struggling to get my daughter to talk about her experience at Ballet West.

18

Nearing the end of my four years with COBRA, it remains difficult for me to reconcile the effectiveness of teams like this in tackling a terrible scourge with the traumatising impact on predators' families. Suspects are not given the assumption of innocence that is theirs by right and hunters don't always get it right (for example, in cases of mistaken identity) and occasionally act on insufficient evidence. While hunters claim that stings aren't intended as punishment, predators disagree: to be publicly exposed as a paedophile is far worse than being arrested by the police, often discreetly, and given a prison sentence.

This leaves the police in a bind: they rely on citizens to help keep children safe and yet cannot be seen to legitimise paedophile hunting as one form of citizen activism. Where they make arrests as the result of stings, they face a CPS who must be satisfied that the evidence is watertight if it is to merit prosecution and, in the many cases where the evidence fails the test, hunters will be left yet more determined to nail those they suspect are protected by corrupt law enforcement.

This isn't to say that police efforts do not also harm the public on occasion. For example, in 1999, British police created Operation Ore, based on information received from US law enforcement on users of a website that reportedly featured child pornography. The police then prosecuted the users that resided in the UK. Operation Ore led to identifying 7,250 suspects, 4,283 homes being searched, 3,744 arrests,

1,848 of the arrests being charged, 493 being cautioned and the removal of 140 children. It also led to an estimated 33 suicides.[1]

Ours is a messy reality and not least because the moral lines aren't clearly drawn. In trying to navigate it, I showed how a narrative reading of hunting might offer us one explanation for why hunters like COBRA's persist with live streaming exposures despite knowing how harmful they can be. Of course, narratives have obvious appeal in helping us navigate complexity: by reducing a morally thorny universe to straightforward rights and wrongs, it creates a fiction in which those far removed from the political process can nonetheless participate in cleaning up the world. That this fiction isn't nuanced matters less than that it is actionable.

In this book, we also considered several explanations for why it is that ordinary citizens take up a role normally reserved for law enforcement: that they do so pragmatically, as a last line of defence in a society where the police do not have the resources to tackle crime effectively; that they respond to a moral scourge and view hunting as a means of participating in a political process designed to restore morality to society; that hunting helps satisfy their existential angst by offering them yet another reason to live while also cementing reputations as guardian angels; and that those who hunt are often themselves survivors of abuse.

To better understand how hunting may partially be a response to childhood trauma, we need more insight into the back stories of hunters and decoys. I asked a few of them to briefly tell their back story.

WINSTON HUNTER

I sort of got to the end of school and the careers teacher told me that I'd either be dead or in prison within the next ten years. That was your future you know prison or dead by the time you're twenty-five, and so, as a young 16-year-old, I took to the road for a couple of years, you know, trying to find myself. When I came back, I remember saying to my dad that I wanted to be a social worker. My dad was ex-military, my brothers served it in the military at the time and since I had nothing, no qualifications, no A levels, no O levels, no GCSEs, no nothing, and my dad told me social workers were left-wing hippies, I inevitably ended up joining the military too.

When I was a child there was no internet but there were predators, and I remember being in a scout group and getting jealous because some of the staff were paying more attention to certain kids and I wondered what they were doing that for. Then I realised that all those getting special treatment were an only child or had no father, you know, that kind of thing, and then it kind of dawned on me that this must be my first exposure to predators. They left me alone because I was six foot four, my big brother was six foot something, you know, and an aggressive type.

I think about that quite often.

Then, years later, I had a deputy at the university where I work, and one day he appeared in an online sting video accused of grooming a child. At the university there were a couple of cases previously where people were arrested so, you know, I'd experienced colleagues being caught by the police. But this was a guy who I was working with and to find out he was a predator knocked me for six. I couldn't handle it. I trusted this man. I remember speaking to my wife about it and my wife at the time was watching a lot of these stings on Facebook and then, one day, she found him being lit up by a team, and it was COBRA. I thought that the way COBRA handled themselves was very professional. And so, I started watching a few of the other teams that are out there, and some I didn't like at all. They were very aggressive, you know, and that's how we get a reputation for being vigilantes. So, my wife decided to start decoying for COBRA, and she'd be sitting there doing her decoying and then, when they were ready to sting the predator, they invited her to come along.

After her first sting she was buzzing, and by the time I first met Jay and Winston they already knew that I was a good guy. Anyway, I said, if you ever need any help, just give us a shout. And so a week or so later, Jay rang me and said, would you like to come out and help provide security. So, going to my first sting and it brought back memories of these scout leaders and of my colleague and I worried about how

I might feel emotionally towards the predator. Thing is, I felt nothing at all. I didn't feel hostility or sympathy or empathy. I just saw someone who was ruining the lives of other people, including his own family. The police came, took him away, and I drove home, and I thought to myself, you know what, that wasn't what I was expecting. I was expecting to feel something more.

I do it not because I'm a survivor, though I know some in the team are, but it is important to me. So, it's not because I've suffered or I'm a survivor. It's nothing like that. It's just a case of wanting to do some good. It's something that I can do that doesn't hurt anybody. And then there is a camaraderie and, well, you know, I enjoy it. I'll be honest with you.

I guess sometimes that can be quite exciting, you know, when you've got a hostile crowd building up during a sting and us trying to get them to understand why we're protecting the predator and how their actions can jeopardise everything. At other times, there's no struggle at all. No one knows we've even been there. Then there are just long periods of nothingness, of driving, of waiting, all for a few minutes of adrenaline when you finally catch that person and don't know how they're going to react.

I think the most surprising sting was where the predator thought he was meeting the child at night, and it turned out he had six knives on him. He could have struck out at us, but he didn't. He wasn't aggressive. But the fact that he had six knives on him meant it could have been a lot worse. And, you know, when I know that we're going after a predator that has been speaking to a real child that increases my desire to get them, even if it meant watching his house from a bush for twenty-four hours in the rain, I'd do it, you know. If we think it's a real child, it increases our desire to stop them. So, yeah, if it's real children – and I think I could speak for quite a lot of us – we want to get predators off the streets as soon as we can. And even if they've been talking to decoys only, I think you'd have to be stupid to think that they're not also talking to real children.

When I look at the chats, I no longer see the predator as a person. I see a bully. I see someone who preys on innocence;

on kids that don't understand what's going on. And so then the predator believes that it's their job to teach kids, you know, what a penis looks like: hey, this is my penis, and look at how fantastic it is, you know. And it does get to you when you think he thinks he's talking to a 12-year-old and thinks it okay to send her images of his penis or asking her to touch herself and do this or that. So then I think, I'm going to show you what control really looks like. And so we sting him, and I kind of look forward to being there when we take all that control away from him.

My biggest fear is that we lit up someone who is innocent, you know, and that's why I'm not keen on chat logs where we sting after 12 hours or 24 hours because they can easily say they were drunk and sobered up the next day, and so you need to give them time to digest what they've done and can decide to delete the talk or walk away. It's like: I started talking to this young girl who's 8, and then when I woke up Saturday afternoon, I thought: what have I done? I'd never sting that guy, you know, because we all make mistakes. There's a difference between making a mistake over an eight-hour drinking session, like putting a traffic cone on your head and running down the street naked, and continuing to talk to a child for two weeks and getting off on it.

I'm not a huge fan of lighting them up live because there's always that fear that they're innocent. I think the minute you put someone's face out there that person's life is ruined, even if they end up being found innocent. And for me, that would be one of the most devastating things we could ever do, you know. I'd rather let a predator walk away than light someone up who was innocent because no matter how many apologies you put out afterwards, they're done for. So, we don't sting unless we are 100 per cent sure that, you know, we've got the guy. And even then, if we turn up and they got obvious learning difficulties, we don't light them up. But I have no problems – and I'll be quite honest – I have no problems if a predator was hanging himself and all that. That's his decision. He chose to go down that road.

LENNY HUNTER

I took my granddaughter to the fair last week, and she wanted to go on the trampoline, the ones that they can bounce on, and obviously the man had to put a safety belt on her and you can imagine me, just him doing that, my eyes are on him watching everything that he does. I don't trust no one.

It started when I was 14 and in a children's home, and while I was there, I was raped. And then another girl was harmed, and the home closed. What happened is that we used to have friends come over and we would hide them in the wardrobe when workers came to check our rooms so that our friends could stay overnight. We all did it all of the time. And then one night, one of the boys had one of his friends stay over and he came into my room. When I woke up, I had bruises and bitemarks everywhere. And so, I decided to foster children, and did so for twenty years, and for teenagers in particular because nobody wants them. Nobody wants teenagers. They're hard work. And then one of my foster kids talked to me one evening and she was like, oh my God, did you hear about that children's home where those girls were raped? And so years later, everyone's still talking about this, about what happened at the children's home I was at. I didn't tell her that I was one of those girls.

LINDA DECOY

I remember being pregnant when watching a sting on Facebook of a man on my street, only about 200 yards from where I was sat in my living room, and I suddenly thought that I wanted to do something too, to protect my children and those of others. And so I created a fake profile of a young girl, went on an adult website and within minutes was contacted by a man. The chat became sexual very quickly and I didn't know what to do and so contacted a hunting team to ask for advice. They read the chat and told me to come join their team, and so I did. And by doing more of this I realised how much of this was happening and how horrible it is that people think it is okay to do this online. And then I remembered how I was abused myself by my neighbour's son, and how I didn't tell anybody and so nothing ever came from that. So doing this kind of helps me get over that.

And one of the predators I decoyed for was Nigel who killed himself. I was the child decoy, and his chat was alarming because he talked about how he abused his grand-daughter. And he just made it sound very natural that he did this with her. He was horrible and it angers me that he decided to take his own life rather than let others deal with what he'd done to them. And then we got these messages from a family member, and she wasn't upset. She just said matter of fact that he'd killed himself last night.

And then we've got girls who are very young and don't mean to be on a chat, but a pop-up invites them and the press a button and someone's talking to them. I remember this girl who was about six and didn't know what she was doing and so the predators had this girl do all kinds of stuff, you know, things like handstands and then telling her it's hot and why not change into a pair of shorts. And she didn't think anything of it. And then her images get passed on all over the internet. That really does play on my mind and especially when I think of my own children. In fact, I'm speaking to a predator right now who openly told me he's been to prison and called himself a paedophile and told me that he went to jail because he had sex with a 13-year-old girl. I asked him if it was scary in jail and he said yes it was, that it was full of robbers that don't value life. You know, I don't think he thinks that what he's done is not valuing a child's life. He doesn't think that way. And that makes me angry: that they don't think this is a problem but a sexual preference. That's it's like someone being gay or bisexual. But it's not. It just isn't.

SCOTT HUNTER

I remember wanting to make a donation to COBRA to help support the work they do but was told that wasn't the done thing. I just thought, These guys aren't paid to do any of this and I'd be happy to contribute something. When I realised I couldn't make a donation, I tried finding out which the most effective teams were and ended up contacting COBRA. They did a lot of stings in my area.

I'd never done anything like it before. I'm 38 years old, got four kids and worked as a stockbroker in the City for twenty years. My wife is a Cambridge graduate and helps run a hedge fund. I have no history of abuse whatsoever, and actually enjoyed my childhood. I went to private school, loved growing up and had great fun at school. I think that if you've been given good luck in life then you should try and give something back. Then I realised there are some crossovers between being a broker and a hunter – you need to be quite a confident person for both – and so that's how I got involved. I really liked the way Jay set up the team. They all have a pretty broad understanding of the law – of what you can and can't say – and aren't trying to get predators worked up too much. That said, in my opinion abuse against children is the worst crime you can commit. It is worse than murder. It really is.

I've probably been on about a hundred stings now and caught, I think, 87 predators, and my experience with police of 95 per cent of these stings have been positive. They've been respectful and engaged. For the other 5 per cent, the experience wasn't bad but just kind of fits within the normal range of people in their day-to-day work. Every now and then someone's going to have a bad day. At the grassroots level, I don't think police are against hunting teams. I'd go so far as to say that for 50 per cent of times I've had police officers give me a fist bump or a thumbs up, and say Thank you for your work, and Keep doing what you're doing.

I think that at a senior level within the police force, they're probably not that keen for several reasons. But the main one, I think, is to save face. I don't think they like the shift in statistics. If you look at the correlation between hunting teams and arrests for sexual crimes against children over the last five years, you'll see that it's massively driven by hunting teams. So, you know, there's an element of egg-on-the-face for a lot of the senior officers.

Of course, it's impossible for police to have the amount of resources they need to do this to the degree we do. We are free labour for police. If you think that there are probably thirty people within COBRA of which twenty are active, and that there's maybe fifty proper hunting teams in England, think of the sheer manpower involved. It'd be completely unfeasible for police to run that level of investment. So I don't judge them. I don't get angry with them.

As I became more involved with COBRA I told Jay that I needed to see the chatlogs. I needed to be 100 per cent certain that the person had committed a crime. Once you've seen the severity of what we do – the impact on girlfriends and wives and kids – you know this isn't just messing about. What we do is actually very serious. And so my preference is for stinging men who actually tried to meet a child. They will actually take a train to go and meet a child. They are probably the ones talking to real children as well. Then there's those who are probably sat at home talking to two or three decoys. That's not to say they don't need to be processed but, in terms of severity, they're in a different league.

Probably the worst I helped sting was the guy with the six knifes. In his chatlogs he was talking about wanting to hurt children, to stab people. I've now watched the video of that sting about five times, and you can see him confessing that he was going to kill someone; that he was ready to kill people. Driving there I thought we were going to meet just another weirdo, but then he ended up telling us he had lots of knives on him. I am utterly convinced that he would have harmed that child – 100 per cent, well maybe not 100 but 95 per cent certain – and so we did something good that night. And he ended up going to court and pleading guilty.

Then there are others who won't confess, and they really annoy me because you end up going home thinking that you've made a mistake. And then, come to find out three or four weeks later, that they actually plead guilty.

I don't really have any empathy for the predators them-selves. People are responsible for their own behaviour. But I do have empathy for their friends and family and, to be honest with you, I sort of block this out. I just can't get involved with every family member of every sting, you know. I just have to block it out knowing there are people within COBRA whose role it is to engage with them. But it's heart-breaking. Many of them had no idea.

I've brought a bottle of prosecco and a bottle of Hendrick's gin along for my last interview with Saz and Jay. We are sitting in pretty much the same configuration as we did the first time I came over: he at a makeshift desk with Saz and me on the sofa. The animals are just as eager to please, all but the parrot who died a few weeks back.

SAZ DECOY
You know Jack, we are fighting a war where civilians come together to fend for their country all over the world to protect children –

JAY HUNTER
But police won't work with us or them –

SAZ DECOY
They're saying that we interfere in their own investigations. That's lies. In the whole time we've been here we've never stepped on their toes –

JAY HUNTER
Never –

SAZ DECOY
But I don't like when they kill their selves –

JAY HUNTER
In all fairness, he was a coward –

SAZ DECOY
But now when they tell us that 'I'm going to kill myself', I am just praying so much –

JAY HUNTER
He took the easy way out because he knew what was coming –

SAZ DECOY
First time it happened, me and Sarah was both in tears. We both was drinking a lot because somebody killed their selves and even though it's because of himself, it is still because of us –

JAY HUNTER
He was a bad 'un –

SAZ DECOY
And to be fair it helped that the family was okay about it –

JAY HUNTER
It did, yeah –

SAZ DECOY
Even though we never told them he was doing it to his own grandchildren –

19

Insofar as all totalising online worlds are characterised by epistemic certainty, I wonder if hunters can perhaps offer us a microcosm of what we see playing out on a larger scale: the emergence of online communities whose dystopian lifeworlds are based on the authoring of villains that need to be redeemed or eradicated by heroes if a righteous order is to be restored where the vulnerable are protected from insidious threats.[1] While for hunters these villains are paedophiles, for others they might be illegal immigrants or political elites. Those expected to heroically rescue us from these menaces include such populist leaders as Nigel Farage or Donald Trump, or radical activists like Greta Thunberg or Julian Assange. Their efforts are targeted at those who need rescuing, like the white working class or those at risk of genocide or suffering the consequences of war.

This authoring finds powerful expression in conspiracy beliefs, a particularly dystopian bundle of which had been packaged and flogged under the label of QAnon. One of its most curious beliefs is that of a world controlled by Satan-worshipping paedophiles who can only be stopped by Trump (who will mobilise an uprising of the heavily armed faithful) in a coming storm. This storm will clear out all evil forces and restore morality to the world. When, in a 2021 poll, the Public Religion Research Institute asked nearly 20,000 respondents whether they agreed with the statement that 'the government, media, and financial worlds are controlled by Satan-worshiping paedophiles', 15 per cent said they did.[2] Twenty per cent believed that 'there is a storm coming soon that will sweep away the elites in power and restore the rightful leaders', while 15 per cent think that 'because things have gotten so far off track, true American patriots may have to resort to violence in order to save our country'. Republicans are significantly more likely to hold both these beliefs than are Democrats and Independents. If QAnon were a religion, it would be as big as all white mainline Protestants in the US.[3] The claim that the world's political, entertainment and financial elites are at heart unrepentant paedophiles has significantly broadened QAnon's appeal to hunters and their supporters, including in the UK, where authorities recorded 309,652 Q-related tweets between November 2019 and June 2020.[4] The suspicion of paedophiles running the world is perhaps not nearly as significant as the symbolism of an all-powerful elite exploiting and defiling the innocent, and who are more innocent than children?

Conspiracy beliefs aren't mobilised for political ends alone. Religious communities have long peddled them, and still do. One example is Seventh-day Adventists, many of whom still believe in a concerted effort to legislate the enforcement of a Sunday law (spearheaded by the Catholic Church). This would prohibit any religious observance outside it, thus specifically targeting Adventists, who keep Saturday as the day of worship (no mention is made of Jews or Muslims). Many believe that the Pope is the anti-Christ (and the fourth beast in Daniel 7:7) which is dreadful and terrible and has iron teeth and eleven horns, the smallest of which has the eyes of a man and speaks great things. Some also believe that members of the Jesuit order infiltrated their church to challenge and destabilise doctrinal positions. Prophesies of the 'end times', courtesy of prophetess Ellen G. White, still hold sway today in a church with 21 million members worldwide. Seventh-day Adventism has a poor performance history: it cashed in on The Great Disappointment that followed William Miller's failed prediction of Christ's return on 22 October 1844. Miller interpreted the 2,300 prophetic days of Daniel 8:14 as referring to years. He tied these to Daniel 9:5, which provided him with a date to start counting: 457 BC, when King Artaxerxes decreed that Jerusalem should be restored to the Jewish people. Adding 2,300 years to minus 457, Miller concluded that the Second Coming was slated for 1843 or 1844. It took yet more reflection and prayer for Miller to settle on 22 October 1844. The good news spread like wildfire.

Over 100,000 followers sold up to await the Blessed Hope only to be rudely awakened by daybreak. 'It seemed that the loss of all earthly friends could have been no comparison. We wept, and wept, till the day dawn,' one wrote, went for a walk and suddenly 'saw distinctly and clearly that instead of our High Priest coming out of the Most Holy of the heavenly sanctuary to come to this earth ... He for the first time entered on that day the second apartment of that sanctuary.'[5] The predicted date had been correct, Heram Edson had said on returning from his walk, but the event hadn't: God had only moved rooms. Having thus saved the day, he crafted a society out of the Millerite mistake. And that's how the Adventist community took root. Keen to learn from its past, it took to revising its prophecies as necessary so as to never again be upstaged by real events.

In an essay for *The Atlantic*, Megan Garber talks about the risk of living *within* these illusions. She points to Aldous Huxley who imagined movies (called 'feelies') that embraced the tactile as well as visual to become 'far more real than reality', and also to Neal Stephenson's vision of a form of virtual entertainment so immersive that it would allow people, essentially, to live within it. We will binge on it, egged on by algorithms, and form communities within it. It helps us build friendships and even sexual relationships, says *New York Times* columnist Ross Douthat. 'We will become so distracted and dazed by our fictions that we'll lose our sense of what is real,' Garber writes. 'We will make our escapes so comprehensive that we cannot free ourselves from them. The result will be a populace that forgets how to think, how to empathize ... Dwell in this environment long enough, and it becomes difficult to process the facts of the world through anything except entertainment. We've become so accustomed to its heightened atmosphere that the plain old *real* version of things starts to seem dull by comparison.'[6] In a similar vein, *Washington Post*'s Jay Will writes that 'when society is bored by its own comforts, there is a "hunger for apocalypse," a need for great drama that can provide some sense of purpose in life.'[7] And it is true that the uprising on 6 January has, at various times, been explained as a visceral reaction to boredom. As Eric Hoffer wrote in 1951, 'there is perhaps no more reliable indicator of a society's ripeness for a mass movement than the prevalence of unrelieved boredom. In almost all the descriptions of the periods preceding the rise of mass movements there is reference to vast ennui; and in their earliest stages mass movements are more likely to find sympathizers among the bored than among the exploited and suppressed.'[8]

Impatient and desperate for entertainment, we enter a world online where normal rules of behaviour don't apply and we carry on without inhibition, assuming all the while that it involves a low-stakes game and therefore what's the big deal? But, says Garber, it can lead us to treat human beings on the other side of the screen as not human, or not real, at all or, to paraphrase Aldous Huxley, to make us, as one set of people, forget that certain other sets of people are human.[9]

Not discounting the genuine harm done to vulnerable citizens by egocentric, misinformed or callous political leaders, the coordination and secrecy requirements of conspiracy theories appear beyond reach in a world as porous as politics, with its infighting, opportunism, indiscretions and scandals. Looking at the stuff headlining our media, it all feels like a bit of a stretch unless, of course, the media's in on the conspiracy. And this is why arguing with those who hold conspiracy beliefs can feel futile: everything is always exactly as one expects it to be if the conspiracy beliefs are true. That is, it is self-sealing in its logic and self-soothing in its effect.[10] In the case of paedophile hunters, that police are critical of their activities is to be expected for they show police to be incompetent. And even where contradictions are blazingly obvious – such as thinking that politicians are unaware of the scale of child sexual abuse while also believing they are in on it – few seem fazed by the contradictions.

The problem of course is that conspiracy thinking can be compelling in part because it offers us a role in solving a puzzle that, once solved, holds the answers to every possible question, no matter how small or large by bringing into view an internally consistent, simple reality beneath the maddening chaos of everyday life. However, say Karen Douglas and colleagues, in a review paper on conspiracy theories, they cater to two other needs too – and these, I think, are especially relevant to paedophile hunters. People turn to conspiracy beliefs because they feel existentially threatened, as if the ontological rug has been pulled from underneath them. Conspiracy beliefs offer security and a sense of control as it helps us understand the existential predicament we're in. Experiments designed to strengthen people's sense of control have been shown to reduce conspiracy beliefs, while other studies show conspiracy beliefs to be correlated with alienation from the political system and feelings of personal unrest and lack of understanding of the social world.[11]

The *Atlantic*'s Ellen Cushing cites another two studies that bear this out. In the first, a series of small experiments conducted on Northwestern University undergraduates in 2008 found that participants who'd been asked to remember a situation where they felt out of control were then more likely to perceive various types of 'illusory patterns' – that is, to find coherent, meaningful relationships amid randomness: to create superstitions, to believe in conspiracies.[12] A more recent study of 200 Polish college students found that when they were in a state of high situational anxiety – waiting to take an exam – they were also more likely to agree with conspiratorial statements drawing on racist stereotypes about Jews, Germans and Arabs.[13]

The need identified by Douglas and colleagues is tied to the idea of superiority (or one she calls the 'social') or of people having 'the need to maintain a positive image of the self, and conspiracy theories may assist people in maintaining this positive image'. Thus, for example, being in possession of bits of knowledge that no one else has makes one feel unique, and uniquely important. Endorsing conspiracy theories is associated with narcissism, or an exaggerated self-view accompanied by the need for external validation, a feeling of being special.[14] That is why, writes Cushing, conspiracy theories 'are organized by the principle of insiders versus outsiders: Conspiracism makes for a convenient way to blame other people for the ills of the world, and offers the added bonus of making the conspiracist feel smart.'[15]

The appeal of vacuously identifying ourselves in terms of what we distrust or oppose lies not in the power of argument but in the intensity of the passions that it stirs. The narratives that are built on such identifications rely, as Byford wrote, on 'feelings of resentment, indignation, and disenchantment about the world. They are stories about good and evil, as much as about what is true.'[16] In the case of paedophile hunters, the narrative that demands the sanctification of the child as pure innocence and a monstrous evil as its opposite is intricately tied to hunters' lack of moral reflexivity in relation to suspected predators and their family members. Even if the fanaticism and dogged persistence this enables may be required to protect children from predators who are not on the police's radar, it also engages them in a cat-and-mouse dynamic that can have unnecessarily cruel outcomes. In addition to being a tale of trauma, conviction and self-sacrifice, the story of hunters is therefore also one of our darker side.

There is also something curious about our tendency to frame human history along narratives: 'the hero's journey' (aka 'overcoming the monster'), as in *Beowulf* or C. S. Lewis' *The Lion, the Witch and the Wardrobe*; 'rags to riches', as in Aladdin or Charlotte Brontë's *Jane Eyre*; 'the quest', as in Philip Pullman's *His Dark Materials* trilogy or J. R. R. Tolkien's *The Lord of the Rings*; and 'rebirth', as in Charles Dickens' *Christmas Carol* or *The Kite Runner* by Khaled Hosseini.[17] Even if history occasionally falls along one of these narratives – think of James Watson and Francis Crick's discovery of the helical structure of the DNA molecule (the quest), Oprah Winfrey (rags to riches) or Florence Nightingale and the Tank Man (the hero's journey) – such examples remain relatively rare and inspiring for precisely that reason. And perhaps it is the scarcity of and yet need for real-life heroes that accounts for the popularity of comic-book superheroes like Batman, Superman, Wonder Woman and Captain Marvel, who, in turn, provide a template not only for paedophile hunters but also for the Sombra Negra in El Salvador, the New York Initiative, the Guardian Angels and organised groups avenging thefts of motorcycles and bicycles and pets.

Then there are similarities too between the world of entertainment and how hunters choose to conduct themselves. This shows up most clearly in their persistence with live streaming despite being aware of the harm caused, and hunters' interest in eyeballs suggests that the effectiveness of stings is measured partly by entertainment value. That is, stings are intended to be consumed as entertainment much like other forms of reality TV: *The X Factor* or *American Idol*, *Big Brother*, *Keeping Up with the Kardashians*, *The Real Housewives of Orange County* or NBC Dateline's *To Catch a Predator*. While all quite different, they rely to a significant degree on exposing and exploiting human frailty, on pent-up frustration and confrontation and, ultimately, on humiliation.

Moral disengagement within the hunting community is shared with many other epistemically closed online communities, and we already know that it can enable people to inflict terrible suffering on others, paradoxically, in the name of some absolute 'good'. While the online hunting community offers plenty of examples of a belief in a cabal of elites running the world (and who happen to have a soft spot for paedophiles), this could merely reflect how powerless they feel and how enormous the threat of child sexual abuse is. And even if they are often deeply distrustful of formal institutions, they do rely on them to secure arrests and prosecutions.

So how do we proceed from here? Maybe it is only through the societal inculcation of the core values of 'epistemic humility' and 'human dignity' that the contemporary turn to totalising online communities may be halted. Taking these values seriously as the basis for reorganising society on- and offline requires making them much more central to children's education, as well as to political discourse, insofar as this is still possible. Naturally, encouraging greater moral reflexivity in our increasingly mediated society is a grand challenge that has no easy fixes. We already know what does not work: turning up the volume by shouting ever more loudly and making others out to be bigots or fools. If we are to make any progress towards bridging existentially different worlds, we might take a leaf out of the ethnographer's book. To paraphrase the anthropologist Tim Ingold, the first rule of ethnography is to take others seriously, not just by attending to what they say and do but by facing up to the challenges they present to our deeply held assumptions about the way things are, and how to live.[18]

20

Her mum and I have hidden pills and anything sharp in the house. Our daughter hasn't left her bed in weeks, takes her meals upstairs and has begun to hurt herself. I feel at a loss because I do not know how to help her.

One morning she tells me that she was afraid he would come for her. I ask her if he did and feel relief at her response. I know she's hiding things from me. But she says she doesn't want to talk about it anymore.

A friend asks me how I feel about what happened to my daughter and to others in my family, and I don't know what to say in response. I don't know what to say because I don't know what I feel. Where's the clarity of mind that should be mine? Where is the rage I should be feeling?

But not knowing what one feels isn't the same as not feeling anything at all. For inside there is a whirlwind of emotions masquerading as a quiet acceptance, the simplicity and benevolence of which is deeply misleading.

EPILOGUE

I sometimes wonder if we choose our fieldwork or if by some bizarre process it chooses us. For how else do I explain the ways in which the world and I repeatedly collide? This is one of several thoughts on loop as I flick through yet another overnight catch of chat logs netted by paedophile hunters. As always, they feature one-directional dirt lobbing, from predator to child. It's been four years since I began 'hanging out' with one of Britain's most prolific group of hunters. Among the usual mishmash, I find the image of a girl, 11 or 12 and certainly not older. It is a screengrab lifted from a social media platform and made up of two images in conversation across a split screen. In the top half the child leans into the image below, showing neither fear nor confusion about what it is she's looking at. Curly bangs sprout from splayed fingers as her hands support her head. I try to make out what it is that fascinates her so. Then I see it too.

Jesus.

I feel dirty and quickly scroll up to rid myself of the image, if not the memory of it, and work my way through the rest of the chats. It is an early morning ritual that I've never gotten used to and cannot wait to rid myself of. For this is humanity's cesspit – what else is it if it isn't that? – and exposure to it feels like a massive caffeine hit: I feel restless, irritable, too cold or, more often, too warm, my pulse racing. I've become uneasy when in the company of kids not my own when walking our dogs in the park. I worry how any friendliness on my part might be misconstrued by watchful parents clued in on the threat some men pose to children. How I may accidentally come to possess illegal images by virtue of my access to private chatrooms of hunters, even if I explicitly told them I hadn't the stomach for it and nor did they, they promised me. How to gain acceptance within the hunting community, I make promises I cannot not keep, and by keeping to myself, imply agreement with moral or political positions I do not hold. It was never clear to me when I should stand up and when stand down when confronted with views so unlike my own, except of course that it often feels easier to let things pass under the cover of an impartial observer.

I agonise daily over what a vindictive hunting community could do to avenge themselves if upset by anything I say or write about them. I fear reprisals from predators who might remember my face, and yet feel cowardly at the thought of wearing a mask when none of the hunters do, and so I don't. Now I worry about having become complicit in the humiliation on display in confronting suspected paedophiles. About how even while knowing how vile predators can be when talking to kids, to me these humiliations feel cruel, and I take to showering afterwards.

I've come to understand why hunters do what they do and how some of what they do keeps children safe. But I have a hard time reconciling their methods with the suffering caused to the families of suspected predators who, oftentimes, hadn't a clue of what their fathers, partners or sons were up to under their roofs. I've come to see why police cannot be seen to condone hunting even as they acknowledge the positive impact of citizens taking it on themselves to fight crime. I think of how different I feel from hunters and how I dread their world, and yet how very welcome they've always made me feel.

And I've come to share their greatest fear: to stand falsely accused of a heinous crime for the simple reason that others in the community have taken a dislike to you or feel wronged by you. How I have come to learn that, in a social media saturated world, there is no recovery from this. And this remains my biggest anxiety, even today.

I have learned to appreciate how the story of hunters needs to be understood in the context of their own pain.

I have come to see how social media has made it far easier for adults to groom children, but also that social media cuts both ways; that it is now far simpler for adults to catch and humiliate those who do the grooming.

I now wonder if the best way forward would have been to write backwards and own up to a growing discomfort with what I was seeing and took part in. Of how I fell into a moral predicament that grew ever more chaotic because of all the things that happened along the way. Of how those closest to me began to talk about their own abuse and, knowing their abusers were no longer alive, how I said I would find out where they lie and desecrate their graves, but was told that it's best to let sleeping dogs lie sometimes.

I'm left with memories of how I turned to the hunters for help when I worried my own daughter had been abused and how they straightaway said they were happy to oblige, and how their next sting was a tribute to her.

Of how a friend told me about growing up near St Dunstan's Church in Cheam, and how that church had a youth club called The Shed run by a 'warlock'. Of how this warlock organised secret rituals in which he passed his special powers on to the kids, one at a time, on the promise of not telling anyone of the mysteries this involved. Strange thing is, my friend said, that everyone knew he was iffy and yet it wasn't until one of them broke ranks twenty years later that Bill Lambert was finally arrested and incarcerated and, as far as my friend knew, is in prison still.

Of how much of this abuse had not only been systemic, but systemically covered up, and how much of it happened in what should have been safe spaces. Of how Hunter S. Thompson said he'd seen thousands of priests and bishops and even the Pope himself transmogrified into a network of thieves and perverts and sodomites who penetrate children and call it holy penance for being born guilty in the eyes of the church, and captured in a few lines the conviction of many: that child molesters are beyond redemption, worse than the fornicator or rapist, wifebeater or murderer, and fit only to be thrown into the fires of Gomorrah, stripped naked and set upon in the most pitiless, most humiliating, most painful of fashions.[1] Of how Thompson is one hell of a writer.

Of how Mildred said it straight in *Three Billboards outside Ebbing, Missouri* to a priest:

> Y'know what I was thinking about, earlier today? I was thinking'bout those street gangs they got in Los Angeles,

the Crips and the Bloods? I was thinking about that buncha new laws they came up with, in the 80's I think it was, to combat those street gangs, those Crips and those Bloods. And, if I remember rightly, the gist of what those new laws said was, if you join one of these gangs, and you're running with 'em, and down the block from you one night, unbeknownst to you, your fellow Crips, or your fellow Bloods, shoot up a place, or stab a guy, well, even though you didn't know nothing about it, even though you may've just been standing on a streetcorner minding your own business, those new laws said you are still culpable. You are still culpable, by the very act of joining those Crips, or those Bloods, in the first place. Which got me thinking, Father, that whole type of situation is kinda similar to you Church boys, ain't it? You've got your colors, you've got your clubhouse, you're, for want of a better word, a gang. And if you're upstairs smoking a pipe and reading a bible while one of your fellow gang members is downstairs fucking an altar boy then, Father, just like the Crips, and just like the Bloods, you're culpable. Cos you joined the gang, man. And I don't care if you never did shit or never saw shit or never heard shit. You joined the gang. You're culpable. And when a person is culpable to altar-boy-fucking, or any-kinda-boy-fucking, I know you guys didn't really narrow it down, then they kinda forfeit the right to come into my house and say a word about me, or my life, or my daughter, or my billboards. So, why don't you just finish your tea there, Father, and get the fuck outta my kitchen.[2]

Of how a different friend told me that he was 17 and she only 11, and that they didn't last long but that her parents liked the idea of them going out. And how he told me that one afternoon they were outside, and he did what he thought she had wanted him to, and how she then told everyone it never happened, and him telling me that he didn't know whether to feel insulted or relieved.

Of how someone I thought the world of told me he didn't think anything had happened; that he and the boy and the boy's father had been drinking all night and that somehow the boy had ended up in bed with him naked. Didn't recall much the following morning, my friend said, and neither the boy nor his father seemed to mind much, but the boy's mother did mind and called the police, and now my friend is awaiting sentencing. Is this, is his, the face of evil? Didn't expect it to look like his, if so.

Of how I didn't know any of this – hadn't the foggiest of how intertwined my life was with survivors – when arranging to join a team of paedophile hunters. Nor did I know that embedding with Cambridge Boat Race crews twelve years earlier was really an attempt to understand what it means to be a man, and nor that a tour of duty with doctors and nurses during Afghanistan's bloodiest summer was the culmination of a search for meaning in a life that had felt so futile.

Of how Nietzsche said that we must be careful when fighting monsters that we do not ourselves become one.

And of how I cannot decide if I should go ahead and revisit this manuscript with a view to inserting all these things or only some, or none, of them.

And so that's what I mean when I say that our research chooses us more than we it.

APPENDIX
NOTES ON METHODOLOGY

Ethnographies rarely ever live up to expectations of a kiss-and-tell account of the lives of others.[¹] What they do offer are descriptions that, for all their imperfections, genuinely aim to show how a specific group of people experience specific circumstances at a specific point in time at a specific place. The emphasis on 'specific' is of course intentional: it foregrounds the significance of context in understanding how people live circumstances on their own terms. As such, ethnography is a *sensibility* more than a method or recipe. If feeds off the affective charge of a field: the complexly interrelated ways in which human behaviour is tied to experience. Perhaps more than any other approach, it relies on us using our ability to build and sustain relationships and place ourselves temporarily in the shoes of another, as well as on suspending any preconceived notions of how circumstances can be lived meaningfully.

This brief note is for those who'd enjoy a tour of the facilities: a walk-and-talk through the processes that led to the book's findings. While the fieldwork itself was my own work, for the analysis I relied on the help of three colleagues, Jaco Lok, Adrian Marrison and Emily Chiang. Adrian was responsible for hand-coding 356,799 words of private online team chat. Emily (a linguist) independently recoded all the chat using *Sketch Engine* – a suite of software tools for analysing large bodies of text. Jaco played a big role in the theorising process. This book is much better for their efforts and collegiality.

The 356,799-word 'transcript' was taken from a total corpus of over 600,000 words, arrived at by applying temporal cut-off dates (October 2018 to April 2020) to enable a focused exploration of a large sample of our chat data so that our analysis could proceed in parallel to the ongoing fieldwork. These eighteen months of coded team chats spanned 54 private Facebook Messenger rooms. The chatrooms included 2 general-purpose rooms for all members, 10 purpose-specific rooms (e.g., researching, decoying) and 42 predator-specific rooms that members were added to as and when required. My Facebook Messenger app was always on, and I was always on it.

Methodological Challenges

Seeing how difficult access negotiations often are, I was fortunate to find a team that had tired of how they were portrayed by police and the media and keen to set the record straight. It seemed important to them for the public to know that amongst the riffraff of amateurs there were professionals: those who didn't lash out at predators or use racial slurs and wouldn't read out excerpts from chat logs between predator and decoy during live streaming. These were the teams who took pains to find out whether a predator might suffer learning difficulties and, if so, to refrain from live streaming but simply call the police instead. They would soften as soon as a predator admitted to all charges and advise on where to seek help. They refrained from commenting publicly on the stings of others and worked hard to keep their identities secret. They would dismiss people from their team for violating any of the above. These then were 'my' team.

Once access was secured, I was instructed to adopt a 'hunting name' and to delete my personal Facebook profile and create a fake one instead, and to never comment publicly on activities by rival teams. The moniker I chose was 'Jack Lenz', the last name after a particularly mad character in David Foster Wallace's *Infinite Jest* ('Randy Lenz'). I didn't want to adopt the typical 'Hunter' last name as a reminder to all that I was an outsider looking in and choosing a foreign-sounding name ('Lenz') would, I thought, reinforce this impression. Given how nearly everyone takes 'Hunter' or 'Decoy' as their (fake) last name, I would be sure to stand out. It was a moral as much as a methodological decision. Once I'd complied with these instructions, I was told I'd be trained on the job, that is, by coming along for the hunting and the exposures. In due course, they said, I'd be able tell their story free of censorship – and, true to their word, they have not tried to interfere with any of the writing.

Having secured access and ethical approval from my department, I reached out to a national taskforce coordinated by the National Police Chiefs' Council (NPCC) which included all UK police chiefs as well as representatives of the Home Office, National Crime Agency (NCA) and Crown Prosecution Service (CPS). They agreed to share their intelligence in the hope that my fieldwork could help them better understand the motivations behind hunting. This taskforce met twice a year, and I was invited to every meeting. In the interest of transparency, I let the hunters know of my arrangement with the police. They, in turn, hoped that the police might come to appreciate the time and toil involved in pursuing those who are oftentimes not known to the authorities yet pose a threat to children.

Notes from my fieldwork were supplemented with secondary sources. For example, Adrian continually monitored the social media pages of other hunting teams and captured six weeks of data in late 2018 for deeper analysis, such as sting videos, posts, and images hunters shared with followers. Helpful contextual information was also provided by a hunter whose historical archives date back to hunting's inception in the UK in 2013 and contain copies of nearly every sting video and relevant media exposure since then. I also relied on twice-yearly intelligence reports produced by the NPCC, threat assessments produced by the NCA, screenshot WhatsApp chat logs between predator and decoy, sting videos uploaded to Facebook, extensive Facebook data on the wider hunting community, extensive interviewing of police, hunters and others who spent inordinate amounts of time protecting our children online (e.g., Internet Watch Foundation, POLIT), a decoying manual produced by Wolf Pack Hunters, TV documentaries, transcripts from the original NBC Dateline series *To Catch a Predator*, media articles, scholarly output, formal inquiries and government white papers and reports as well as reports by various NGOs charged with keeping kids safe.

Data Analysis

The ethnographer's grasp of a community's 'inner world' is invariably tentative in that, as Clifford Geertz said, we cannot gain access to it through some 'magical intrusion into their consciousness'.[2] Still, one can get a sense of people's experience by interpreting the everyday meanings they make use of in relation to one's own experience of their world. Two qualities are central to this enterprise: empathy – or a willingness to let oneself be educated by others about their world; and doubt – or the refusal to believe that there is only one best way to live a meaningful life.[3] When the relation between a community's lifeworld and its material-symbolic expressions is understood as dialogic, the latter can be interpreted to reveal some important aspects of the former as each defines and illuminates the other.[4] This involves a complex interpretive process of 'getting from [observed] cultural forms to lived life and back again in such a fashion that neither disappears and both are explicated, at least somewhat'.[5] For us, this process consisted of cyclically interrogating the ethnographer's preunderstanding based on their prolonged immersion in the setting against the available data and the relevant literature.[6] Thus, rather than inducing theory through identifying general patterns,[7] we actively used the ethnographer's preunderstanding to orient our analysis, focusing on the contextual authenticity of our reasoning throughout.[8]

Ongoing reflexive self-examination in relation to observations and interpretations is critical to this process. Such reflexivity can reveal that even if empathy is critical to bridging existentially different worlds, it does not also involve approving of all practices that constitute these worlds. Thus, my interpretations are necessarily value-laden, critical of both the terrible child abuse I bore witness to, as well as the dehumanising practices hunters engage in, without ever wishing to suggest that these are somehow comparable. The analysis also inevitably belies the many idiosyncrasies that characterise the lifeworlds of those we study, as much as they do my own: existential projects forged out of circumstances beyond our control (such as our upbringing and our social history) that can nonetheless be lived in a variety of ways.[9] Even though this necessarily limits the generalisability of our findings, I do think that the hunting team I studied shares important characteristics with other hunting teams, as well as epistemically closed, radicalised online communities more generally. The findings reported here are intended to offer a starting point for developing a deeper understanding of the lived experience of such communities.

Puzzling practices act as an entry point. At the early stages of analysis, Jaco Lok (my co-author on two academic articles based on this fieldwork) spent hours over several days in what felt like an interrogation designed to help us get at inconsistencies, conjectures and my own intuitions on what might actually be going on in the data, and what paedophile hunting could plausibly be seen to be a case of. The critical distance this process produces is particularly important in ethnography, where the representations that informants give of themselves may differ from the actual practices they engage in. Our initial discussions produced several key themes, such as the enactment of threat or danger; dehumanisation of targets; mutual caricaturing between hunters and police; and low reflexivity combined with high emotionality. It also prompted us to ask open questions, including: Does the fact that they engage in live streaming necessarily mean that they are driven by narcissistic motivations as per police suspicions? How can hunters believe they are safeguarding children when their actions can jeopardise police investigations?

Such questioning focused our analytical attention on several paradoxical observations that we found difficult to explain based on our knowledge of extant theory and hunters' ostensible concerns. For example, hunters would persistently seek answers from dumbfounded targets unable to provide them; they expressed a lack of faith in the judicial system but deferred to it for convictions; they were clearly bothered by outside criticisms yet made no discernible efforts to increase their legitimacy beyond a narrow group of supporters; they spent an inordinate amount of time monitoring and commenting on other teams rather than using this time to catch more predators; they showed interest in the conviction of their targets, yet failed to educate themselves on laws and methods that might enhance the chances of conviction; and finally, their justifications for live streaming stings did not hold up to even the barest of logical scrutiny.

We tentatively labelled these 'puzzling practices' and decided to use them as a focus for subsequent data analysis – not least as none appeared to be of concern to hunters themselves. This realisation oriented the analysis to uncovering ways-of-being through which the puzzling practices would either make self-evident sense or would be experienced as irrelevant. In other words, even if each of the puzzling practices might be explainable on its own terms (and within the fold of a specific academic literature), we were interested in better understanding the collective lived experience through which all puzzling practices could be better understood. For example, some puzzling practices on their own might be classified as organisational paradoxes[10] or forms of organised hypocrisy[11] that are characteristic of many organisations. However, to us neither of these frameworks appeared well equipped to understand the puzzling practices in terms of different ways of being, feeling, seeing and acting through which none were experienced as particularly puzzling by hunters themselves.

Theorising

The understanding that practice can involve a multiplicity of individual and collective lived concerns[12] that are inseparably tied to the process of authoring identities[13] led Jaco and me to focus our analysis on better understanding the different identities hunters constructed in and through their practices in relation to multiple ways-of-being. This analysis consisted of two parallel components that continuously informed each other. The first involved the sorting of hunting practices by possible motives and related emotions that could help explain them as suggested in the literature or as offered by the police and hunters themselves. Jaco, Adrian and I began by identifying those practices that did, and those that did not, appear consistent with hunters' ostensible motive of protecting children and related emotions of fear, anger and anxiety. We included both practices that functionally served their pragmatic objectives in a direct way (e.g., decoying, recording evidence, calling the police to make the arrest) and those that hunters used to justify them as necessary (e.g., authoring the police as incompetent and enacting the threat of paedophilia as omnipresent). We repeated this process, narrowing the list of practices that were left unexplained as we progressed, by trying to explain remaining practices in terms of moral threats (as prevalent in the vigilantism literature), narcissism (as suspected by police) and psychological trauma (as acknowledged by hunters themselves). We went through these cyclically rather than sequentially, allowing for overlaps and multiple possible interpretations from which our identification of four distinctive ways-of-being gradually emerged: pragmatic, moralistic, narcissistic and traumatic.

Hunters' stark identifications of predators as pure evil, and of the police as incompetent, prompted the second main component of our analysis as it evoked the archetypal narrative of the Hero overcoming a monstrous Evil to protect Innocence.[14] We began wondering whether this narrative frame might be useful for developing a deeper understanding of their lifeworld. We decided to explore this more systematically by coding the chat log data for the multiple identities that hunters authored for themselves and others. For example, people can construct an enhanced identity through positive comparisons against a reference group, as observed in the literature on 'dirty work'.[15] We used both to code excerpts in which a particular actor was (self-)identified. This was done manually as the Facebook Messenger chats contained significant misspellings, grammatical errors, colloquial language, half-finished sentences, a heavy reliance on emojis, and use of inbuilt features such as 'reactions'. We then grouped these codes into distinct identity categories. For example, we categorised the main identity hunters authored for suspected predators as 'evil monsters' based on hunters (a) using a range of dehumanising monikers for their targets (e.g., 'Mr Hardman'), including the frequent literal use of 'evil' or 'monster'; (b) identifying them as 'dangerous' in several different ways (e.g., 'he is going to kill someone in the near future'), and framing the threat they pose as omnipresent (e.g., 'they seem to be breeding in incredibly large numbers'). Adrian took the lead in this three-month process, raising for discussion any instances where he was unsure until agreement on the appropriate code was reached.

We engaged in reflexive discussions about the implications of emerging themes and insights across both components, drawing on our reading (both broadly and deeply) of relevant literature on, for example, vigilantism,[16] dehumanisation,[17] the anthropology of experience,[18] archetypal myths,[19] the role of narrative in organisations,[20] existential anthropology[21] and existential psychology.[22] Two key insights gradually emerged through this creative inferential process. First, through their characterisations of the police (as incompetent), the predators (as evil monsters), the children (as innocent and vulnerable) and other hunting teams (as narcissistic amateurs), hunters also authored related identities for themselves, thus constituting four identity pairs. We then noticed that each of these identity pairs could be directly related to one of the four ways-of-being that emerged from the first component. This synthesis led us to infer 'heroic being' as a fifth way-of-being constituted in the other four, as the identities central to the latter closely mirrored the central characters through which the archetypal hero is narratively defined. For where there are villains, there are victims and those unable to offer the necessary protection. All that is missing is a knight in shining armour.

When They Read What We Write

In my fieldnotes (and in this book) I hoped to retain the linguistic cultural specificities of the hunters. Many of these specificities are in the recorded material (using my iPhone) or in 'sting' videos uploaded onto Facebook or YouTube. I wrote myself into the text on the strong suggestion of my amazing (superhero) editor, Valerie Appleby, who was keen for me to show how I was affected by what I witnessed. It also seemed the correct thing to do methodologically, for it allows the reader to see my own prejudices and foibles at play. For while I tried hard to retain some critical distance throughout, readers will notice where I fell short, and by 'showing up' in the text alongside hunters, I hope to have given readers what they need to draw their own inferences. I am keenly aware of Joan Didion's claim that writers are always selling somebody out, even if they don't wish to.

So, I decided to try something different: to ask Oliver (Wolf Pack Hunters), Saz, Lenny and Jay (COBRA) and Dan Vazjovic (Depute Chief Constable of Bedfordshire Police and chair of the Online Citizen Child Abuse and Exploitation Activist Groups (OCAGs) national taskforce) to write their uncensored replies to the book. I provided them with a draft of the manuscript with the invitation to write a brief response to it: to tell you where I occasionally got it wrong and, hopefully, also where I got it right; to fill in whatever gaps there might be in the text or where there's a risk of misunderstanding; and, more generally, to tell you whatever remains to be said about their world, and their work. You'll find their responses here.

WHEN THEY READ WHAT WE WRITE

Saz (COBRA)

I came into the hunting scene by accident. My husband wanted to join and said it was something we could do and make a difference to the world. Back when we started it was all underground and you never saw any faces of team members. During my first sting I was terrified and thought 'what if they are vigilantes' and 'what if the predators are now hunting the hunters?' I got ready making sure my hair and make-up were perfect! Maybe I did this to distract myself and pass the time, as I don't like walking into the unknown. Jay gave me a hug and told me to trust him and that I will come to no harm. I kept quiet all the way and prayed no one could meet us at the other end.

We were met by a man and introduced ourselves. I wasn't feeling comfortable but Jay was and so I put it down to nerves. We waited a long time for a lady who arrived. She looked me up and down and asked where my mask was. I said that we were not told to wear one, but she was not impressed. I just wanted to go home as my anxiety was escalating and especially when I realised we were only a team of four. What if the sting kicked off? We had no clue what we were doing and oh! My! I'm definitely not a fighter.

Thankfully, we did not catch anyone that night. We walked and drove miles around London, and I built a bond with the lady hunter. Her passion, commitment and drive gave me good grounding for what I was walking into, and she made me feel safe in her company. We remain friends today and I am grateful to her for her advice as it provided the foundations for our own team.

Paedophilia is a subject that makes everyone uncomfortable and within the law they are protected, and courts keep their identity a secret. How is that ethically right? What does that signal to survivors? Should they do the same and keep quiet about their abuse? Because in my opinion that is how it looks because for years people never told a soul and now due to the hunting community, we break the silence. This is something that should have been done years ago.

Hunting is not a cure but a prevention and a deterrent to stop abuse online. The police do not have the manpower or technology since social media has taken every country by storm and is freely available to everyone at every age. Anyone can join and although the apps state an age limit, many children join by stating they are of age by ticking a box. This opens the doors for children to be abused in their own homes, and how is this right? These children are our next generation need protection, and why should we sit back and do nothing? The Internet now gives you the power to make a difference! No more silence! We are making a stand against child abuse! Educate your children to come forward without fear of retribution and show them the videos of stings, that this is real life! This could happen to them. Prevention and education are the key moving forward in keeping kids safe.

I was under no illusions when we agreed to participate in Mark's research and that his personal perception would not be to advocate for hunting. However, he might be the key in getting teams regulated. That was my motivation for accepting: to move the hunting community forward. Teams are penalised for how we conduct ourselves, evidence gathering etc. So, why don't police educate us all, and train us to their standards, so we can be united? My question is if hunting is immoral. If it is unjustified then why is it not banned? In my opinion it's because we are making a difference but there is still a poor perception of hunting teams. Even this book highlights the perception of people's thoughts and feelings on hunting. This is a hard read at times, but it is a dark subject to take on, and especially the impact on the families. For me that was the hardest part of my role to undertake as this is not a game because of the destruction we cause to them. I can personally say on behalf of all teams that we are truly sorry for the aftermath on you and especially to the families that never got answers because the predator took their own life.

Paedophilia is a sexual attraction to children and still today we do not have answers as to why. The devastation it causes to children and throughout their adult life is the destruction of their psychological and physical wellbeing. You can think it a sexual orientation. However, it's an unwritten code in humanity to protect children. Some would say a natural instinct. Yet predators continue to carry out this act even as there is no justification for their wickedness.

You could argue about the way the hunting community carries out exposures online. However, the fact remains that the predators made their choices and are solely responsible for their premeditated actions. The fact that they are talking to decoys at times should not be a factor as they believe they are talking to real children when carrying out sexual sexual acts online and, in some cases, in person.

This book focuses on hunting using decoys. However, if all cases involved real children, would your judgement of the hunting community change? Naturally, as humans we pass judgement in terms of what think is right and wrong, and the severity of the crime and the punishment that deserves. The fact we all unconsciously look at predators' characteristics and social status on live streams influences your perception of the crime committed, and in some cases your own personal emotions can blind you to the fact that this is a premeditated crime, when you strip the case down to its bare bones and remove all emotions. This is how our justice systems works, using only the evidence before the court in passing a sentence.

I can only speak for myself regarding hunting and how COBRA UK conduct themselves and my own conduct when confronting a predator. We take pride in what we are trying to accomplish as activists and educate ourselves on the law. From the time we started, I would agree in today's society that the way some teams conduct themselves is not acceptable. However, this again is a personal perception, and they may feel the same about our team. My only concern is that of teams putting their identity out online for whatever reason and there will be repercussions as in America one hunter has already been shot.

Times have changed from when we first started, and we were known as 'vigilantes'. Police now identify some teams as 'activists' instead. This is a positive shift in that many teams are on the same path as us. Over time, we have educated parents, schools, and have protected and prevented real children from abuse and have broken the silence around child abuse. Thus, the evidence clearly indicates that the presence of the hunting community is having a positive effect on reducing child abuse overall, as predators are aware of our online presence. In conclusion, they make the choice to act on their impulses and are responsible for their own actions as well as the impact they have on their family and friends.

The hunting community is an easy target for deflection of anger, but don't lose sight that children are the heart of this crime. It is time for civilians to take a stand like many do for a change in society, and even if paedophilia is a uncomfortable reality. In regard to the police, we fully respect them, but know they have the power to stop hunting or to regulate teams. I myself cannot comprehend why neither has yet been done. Only they can answer this question. Police have the power for the hunting community to move forward united or to stop hunting forever.

Lenny (COBRA)

Decoys are the heart of the hunting community and join for their own reasons. Yes, some are survivors, but the majority are not, and together we fight for change. Undertaking this role comes with high demand of your time as well as a significant mental and emotional toll. This is a 24/7 job for 365 days a year as it is the predators who control the conversation. Many decoys leave due to the pressure of all this.

You would think Christmas would be a time to take a break and wind down but for decoys this is not the case. It is our busiest time of year as this is when children receive new devices as gifts. No matter how many times our team leader says: 'time out ladies', in the back of our heads we're all saying: 'that's not going to happen'.

Many people believe we set up a profile and then simply get on with the conversation, but this isn't all there is to decoying. There is so much more to it as we need to be trained in safeguarding. We do this using an online course which gives us a recognised qualification. Understanding the law and working within it gathering your evidence from start to finish is critical to securing arrests and convictions. Then you have to imagine yourself as a child, meaning that you have to have a believable background story, need to be aware of trends, popular music and films as well as be on top of school hours and school holidays in the area where your decoy lives.

To be honest in COBRA most of our work is not seen by the public because we monitor live applications to safeguard real children who are at risk of predators pretending to be online 'fans'. We do this not just in the UK but across the world and have a network of safeguarders in other countries that we work with for a quick response to make sure children are safe.

Here's what a typical day for decoys is like: I wake up, say 'good morning' to the predator I'm talking too unless they already made contact. I then put the kettle on and get my kids their breakfast. 'Ping! Ping!' goes my phone so I answer while juggling to get the kids dressed. 'Ping! Ping!' There we go again. I answer halfway through getting my own kids ready for school. Now I must also get myself dressed. 'Ping! Ping!' The predator's need for attention is relentless.

I get the kids in the car and the phone keeps 'pinging'. I've come to hate that sound but feel guilty for this because in talking to me it means he's leaving a real child alone. I manage to free myself up for an hour by telling the predator that class is starting. I know I must keep to a schedule of school times for breaks, etc, as they even try to talk to the child while they are at school.

I pick up my kids and 'Ping! Ping!' here we go again. I am now talking to the predator while juggling getting dinner ready for the kids and listening to them talk about their day at school. After this I have a couple of hours to sit and watch a movie with the kids though I find it hard to concentrate based on what the predator has told me during the day.

I try to make up an excuse while bathing the kids but still hearing the phone ping a hundred times because of how impatient some predators are. If you don't answer quickly, they block you and move onto another child.

I put my own kids to bed and sink into the sofa exhausted, pick a movie and try to chill only for the phone to start pinging again seeing as night-time is the busiest period of all. Boy, I'm tired, but if the monster wants to play, how can I put my phone down?

I have fallen asleep with the phone in my hand. Predators have kept me awake until 2am. I lie there and think I just need some sleep as the kids will be up in 5 hours. The alarm clock goes off and the day starts all over again. And then when one predator has been picked up, you're halfway through another already. You don't even have time to process the aftermath.

Every case is different. And every case has an impact on you. The justice system is slow on sentencing, and it can take up to 5 years before you get closure. The police want decoys to hand over their evidence but take too long to act and won't always communicate after the evidence has been handed in, and unless it involves a real child, they may not do anything for weeks or months, if they do anything at all. That's why we use hunters to carry out our work.

It is clear from the sentences our predators receive that this is not low-level crime. Therefore, we will continue with our work to keep children safe online.

Oliver (WOLF PACK HUNTERS)

Are LGBT people and their allies a psyop to groom children into gender transition? Are celebrities kidnapping children to drink their adrenochrome? These are both stories that people have repeated in recent years. These are stories I heard in the paedophile hunting community. Did Jewish people use the blood of non-Jewish children in hermitic rituals? Did Marie Antoinette sexually abuse her own son?

In all four examples, 'undesirable' people are recast as child abusers. The people who tell these stories position themselves as the saviours of children and combatants against perversions. In a world run by imaginary elite lizards, everyday 'normal' people are called into conflict against them, to restore 'traditional moral values' – like the men in black who recently goose-stepped adjacent to an anti-trans rally, saluting and carrying flags that demand we 'Destroy Paedo Freaks'.[1]

In 1980s Britain, where I grew up as a queer child, it was our prime minister Margaret Thatcher who insisted on a return to children learning 'traditional moral values'.[2] The ensuing climate of homophobia led to parents abandoning their own queer children or 'sentencing' them to schools silent on living safe lives during the rise of the ongoing HIV/AIDS epidemic. In the card game 'British Nonces',[3] Thatcher is listed at number one in a deck of historical 'nonce enablers', for her alleged complicity in covering up child abusers in her own cabinet. Let alone the young people she sentenced to parental eviction or early deaths at the hands of the virus.

I must be careful of not falling into imagination myself, so let me tell a short story of first-hand Thatcher-era experience. A queer child I knew at school, my friend, was expelled from their own home for homosexual 'transgressions'. Abandoned, they apparently had no choice but to move into the home of a much older man, where sexual exploitation was the exchange for 'safe' shelter. It is bigotry, not acceptance, that directs children into abusive situations. In the 2020s, with the current Conservative government waging a war on trans-youth, how will we not expect this cycle of abandonment and abuse to reoccur?

In Mark's text, he draws from Hobsbawm on 'Bandits', and their self-conception as restorers of traditional morality. But who holds and directs the idea of 'traditional moral values'? Is it the politicians and professionals, that some paedophile hunters disavow, or the everyday 'non-professionals' that inspired the early wave of paedophile hunters? Are the latter unaffected by the speech and ideas of the former, that some claim to fight against? In his book *Witchfinders: A Seventeenth-Century English Tragedy*, Malcolm Gaskill explores the atmospheric link between the social unrest leading to the English civil war (stemming from politicians and professionals) and the re-emergence of witch-finding in Britain[4] (led by everyday 'non-professionals'). Sometimes people think they are challenging power, when they are in fact led by it into turning on their own. It seems valuable to consider the rise of paedophile hunting in connection with the social unrest of the austerity crisis in Britain and beyond.

Despite any liability for trauma that could be directed towards the politicians and others charged with protecting us, as Mark's experience records, allegiance to 'old power' is rife in paedophile hunting. Consider the references to Armistice Day, admiration for the Royal Family, or the number of teams (including Wolf Pack) utilising the Union Jack in their logos and badges. During my own extended engagement with the hunting community, I sometimes came across teammates with swastika flags on their social media, or sometimes even hanging in their homes. It was the homophobic and transphobic accusatory posts within the community that partly enticed me to initially consider my involvement. To a greater degree this is because, for years since my homophobic Thatcherite schooling, I was filled with, and excited by, the shame and rage of internalised homophobia.

Mark's text questions how I came to co-found Scotland's premiere paedophile hunting team, but in my practice as an artist, I had already mobilised shame and rage for years without acknowledging its presence. It began at age 20, following Claire Bishop publishing her essay 'Antagonism and Relational Aesthetics'.[5] In her text Bishop draws upon Laclau and Mouffe's publication *Hegemony and Socialist Strategy: Towards a Radical Democratic Politics*[6] and applies its critique to late twentieth-century 'Relational Aesthetics' artists, famous for creating social spaces for 'micro-utopias' of people to come together. Bishop, via *Hegemony*, characterises those outside the utopia, those who antagonise the consensus, as preventing political stagnation and maintaining the conflict vital to democracy. My young, traumatised brain misshaped this argument and projected upon it the conclusion that community was suspicious, and that cruelty served a purpose. The context in which I first entered art was through this combined will to antagonism and the backdrop of individualistic artists of Cool Britannia, the latter popularised by Charles Saatchi, the 'adman' behind Thatcherite government's own promotional materials. By the time I entered hunting formally in 2017, I had been working as an antagonistic, individualistic artist for over a decade. My speciality was taking seemingly hopeful gestures and exposing their potentially underlying cruelties. Paedophile hunting, for me, was my first foray into community-led antagonism – and into the idea that this gesture could heal my own shame and rage through catharsis.

Towards the end of her video essay 'Cringe', Contrapoints (aka Natalie Wynn) draws attention to fellow trans YouTuber Blaire White's obsession with transgender predators. Through her observations Wynn demonstrates a tendency of some marginalised people to attempt to exorcise their own hurt through redirecting it towards other people within their own demographic – 'it feels good to be the judge rather than the judged'.[7] As mentioned above, I felt a similar (although unacknowledged) urge in my move towards paedophile hunting. The pleasure of being part of a group of 'normal people', leading the charge, rather than being subject to it. As a decoy I always played the role of a young boy and used queer dating apps such as Grindr as my hunting ground. When the chat log was ready, I would hand these unsuspecting men over to a community where I knew there remained the age-old right-wing suspicion that all gay men are predators. Amongst several women I decoyed with, I observed a similar interest in catching a woman – a rare prize and gender shocker. And of course, it was women that I mostly decoyed with, as my experience of the hunting practice showed a reinforcing of traditional gender essentialism. Women passively gathered predators and men actively hunted them down.

My main discovery over the five years I ran with Wolf Pack was that many of my teammates, people I would have feared would have bullied me at another time, were also often filled with shame and rage from their own childhood traumas. Slowly I began to realise that hunting itself is a practice perfect for reconfirming one's own shame and rage. These emotions are directed at the predators during stings, and at other teams or community members during downtime. There is no healing through catharsis, just an endless reconfirming of a suspicion that the world is critical and cruel. This conception becomes a self-fulfilling prophecy and during my hunting years, I lost my home, my career and eventually most of my non-hunting relationships.

There is a worrying portent that in most paedophile hunting cases, the vulnerable children being saved are imagined. Although paedophile hunting inarguably captures real abusers, my main retrospective concern is the possibility for the practice to act as a model for more extreme movements, and to encourage the gathering of the majority to displace their imagined victimhood onto minority targets, to blame scapegoats for systemic failures. Consider how easily the hunting technique was adapted in Putin's Russia by 'Parents of Russia' and 'Occupy Paedophilia', two teams who lured, exposed and ritually humiliated closeted queer Russians for social media videos[8] – beating them and forcing them to drink urine on camera because they supposedly present an imagined threat to children. In one video they kidnap and use these terrorising techniques on a 15-year-old boy accused of being gay.[9] Now consider the new calls for a return to 'traditional moral values' coming from various far-right movements in Western countries. In the USA, Chaya Raichik, owner of far-right social media 'Libs of Tik Tok', accuses and exposes imagined 'groomer' teachers, children's hospitals performing imagined gender affirmative care, and school libraries stocking imagined pornography. Several American news outlets have recently published articles correlating these exposures with subsequent real threats to individual's lives and bomb-threats to those same children's hospitals and schools.[10] In the UK, Kellie-Jay Keen-Minshull, leader of the anti-trans rallies 'Let Women Speak', imagines trans-women as paedophiles[11] and imagines them entering women's toilets to leave semen all over the walls.[12] This is the same Kellie-Jay Keen-Minshull who has encouraged armed civilian men in America to police toilets designated for the use of women and girls, including school toilets.[13] All of this is in the name of saving children. If you challenge these groups or their beliefs the response online is always the same: 'Ok, groomer'. I recognise this response, because it is the same one regularly delivered to critics of paedophile hunting.

During the summer of 2017, paedophile hunting groups began to divide themselves into groups of professionals (represented in this book by COBRA) and self-styled 'unprofessional vigilantes' (represented in this book by Wolf Pack). The pinnacle of thematised unprofessionalism was marked in Autumn 2017 by Internet Interceptors, an early team often indicated to be the first to live stream, who forced one of their predators to play a game of 'Nonce Bingo'. In this game the predator gives all the tired old excuses the audience has heard a thousand times, for each excuse the audience tick boxes on their bingo card. For example: 'I only came to tell her not to meet people from the internet', or 'I didn't know he was underage'. But, as anyone with experience of watching stings will know, most hunting teams also replicate similarly repeated accusations. It is possible to play 'Hunter Bingo'. For example: 'If this was my child, we wouldn't be meeting you with a camera', or 'If you don't calm down, you'll go on the floor'. The game highlights how both predators and hunters have become stagnant. Tradition is comforting for those stuck in shame. The game is fixed, nothing can change. Anyone who disagrees with the established values is at best a 'nonce apologist' or at worst a groomer. Teams who attempt to break away from the script are ousted as the antagonists of the community. Because they explore a different way of being, they are imagined to be 'not in it for the children'.

For now, I am lucky. It took time, but these realisations of shame and rage, displacement and stagnation, tradition and imagination, dawned on me. Since leaving that world behind I have begun what is known as 'the real work': talk therapy, yoga, pranayama, EMDR, CBT and Emotional Freedom Technique. I found a new job working for a charity that provides creative experiences for marginalised people and became the voluntary leader of a community group for neurodivergent LGBT people. Most importantly,

I am working on healing by creating opportunities that show the real world as kind and benevolent. Hunting does not work as a healing practice because it prizes an imaginary of universal suspicion. Clinging to tradition keeps us trapped in the past where most of us were hurt, and hurt people really hurt people. Restoring and internalising trust in new ways of being is central to real, resilient healing.

Police

In 2018 I was asked by the then Chief Constable of Norfolk Police, Simon Bailey, to further develop the approach that policing took to the growing phenomenon of so called 'paedophile hunters'. The whole of policing was and remains resolutely committed to tackling child abuse. From my experience of leading the police teams that go undercover to root out the most horrendous predators online, I have a strong understanding of the work our dedicated professional officers and staff undertake to catch more and more high-harm offenders. Over recent years, we have successfully argued for more and more stringent sentencing guidelines. Despite more arrests and longer sentences, our best efforts alone do not meet the scale of offending. We need continued resource investment, technological innovation and importantly the help of industry and the public. In an emerging popular narrative, so called 'paedophile hunters' could potentially offer support to policing in our fight to tackle child abuse. And yet, back in 2018, I had a deeply felt concern about the activities of these groups. It is in this context that my contact with Professor de Rond developed. I welcome the publication of this book and thank Mark for the insight he has provided.

Policing no longer refers to these groups as 'paedophile hunters'. We would not support the notion of 'hunting'; the mission of a criminal justice system is to bring offenders to justice, not to ritualistically humiliate or exercise control or behave as hunters have themselves described as 'thugs looking for mob justice'. Nor is the term 'paedophile' appropriate in the context of these activists. Having seen so many examples where groups have targeted vulnerable adults who had no prior sexual interest in children, I remain unconvinced that all of the subjects of stings can be properly described as paedophiles. For this reason, policing now refers to 'hunters' as Online CSE Activist Groups (OCAGs) – members of the public who collectively work as activists in the arena of online facilitated child abuse.

Protecting children is a policing priority; every month we arrest or interview more than 1,000 people for offences relating to child sexual abuse and protect more than 1,000 children from harm. We do need the public's help in this fight and there are many ways concerned citizens can support child protection: raising money for relevant charities, volunteering for organisations that work legitimately in this area or even taking the step to join us as a Special Constable. When members of the public decide that the correct course of action is to become a 'hunter', I worry that they have no way to control the risks their activities create. They can't safeguard children, they can't stop offenders from destroying evidence, they can't stop offenders notifying other people who they are in touch with and importantly they have no means to support the innocent people wrapped around the alleged offender. Knowing all these risks and yet persisting with what they do makes one wonder what their motivation is? OCAG's activities are not targeted. A lack of operational insight means that they often operate in chat rooms where there might be offending but where what offending there is, isn't as grave as that which takes place elsewhere. As unpalatable as it is to say, policing has to target its activity at the most harmful cases and then use other tactics to disrupt lower-level offending. When OCAGs bring cases to us relating to, for example, a vulnerable adult with additional learning needs, we will deal with that case whilst pausing the other investigations we have ongoing.

The police will always review evidence and investigate allegations brought to them; however, the standard of evidence that is gathered is often poor and there are issues with disclosure and the way in which the groups share that evidence. Some evidential issues can cause cases to collapse. Issues with evidence include poor disclosure and refusing to allow phones to be seized by police for evidence to be examined. This book explains the motivations of activists in this regard but that is of no matter when trials collapse. Some groups provide poor quality evidence that does not provide a realistic prospect of conviction and some groups do not follow laws and regulations around gathering evidence so the information they provide is unusable in court. Because these groups operate without the skills and knowledge of police officers, it can allow sophisticated offenders to destroy evidence before it is seized by police. Some of the activity of these groups is a cover for their crimes, like blackmail and extortion. There is no way of making sure that these groups act on reliable evidence, and we have seen instances of the wrong people being targeted (like vulnerable adults and paediatricians). Activists sometimes put a family home address online leading to innocent third parties being the victim of abuse and harassment.

Through Mark's work, I have had the opportunity to meet activists face to face and to understand their motivations. I am sure that amongst all the activists there are many people whose motivations are honourable. There are, sadly, also many examples where activists are simply using their group as a cover, or justification, for the use of violence, extortion and gratuitous public humiliation.

For that reason, the position of the police in England and Wales is that we do not endorse these groups and will not work with them. I thank Mark for his work in this area. I thank the public who help us to fight child abuse. And finally, I pay tribute to the many men and women working in law enforcement and the intelligence community across the country and internationally who strive tirelessly in the fight to stop abuse and to bring abusers to justice.

ACKNOWLEDGEMENTS

I owe this book to the open-mindedness and wonderful camaraderie of Saz, Jay, Lenny, Steve and other COBRA members, and of course to Oliver who made the introduction and taught me much of what I know about the hunting community. This book simply wouldn't be here at all if not for their generosity, and I know that parts of it weren't easy for them to read. There are others within this community who were instrumental in making introductions, and you'll have recognised yourself in the text. Then there are those family members who found themselves inadvertently at the sharp end of hunting and are deeply sceptical of it and brave enough to share their experiences. This book is for all of you.

Likewise, I appreciate the strong support of Dan Vazjovic, Neil Sloan, Sarah Robertson and many others in law enforcement who work hard (and often thanklessly) to keep our streets and our online worlds safe. I am lucky to have colleagues who are supportive of my fieldwork (or appear to be in any event), and Tamsin Varney in particular.

My long-time co-author and friend, Jaco Lok, did much of the heavy lifting analytically – he's particularly good that way – while Adrian Marrison, as my then PhD student, spent months coding the chat logs by hand. Emily Chang, a linguist at Aston University, subsequently recoded everything using a specialised software program, and it is to Adrian's credit that the computer-generated analysis correlated so strongly with his own coding. I appreciate the careful editing of a prior journal publication by Tammar Zilbert and three anonymous reviewers for the *Academy of Management Journal*.

That the text reads better than it otherwise might is due to the efforts of my wonderful friend Karina Isabel, my exceptional editor Valerie Appleby and copy-editor Kay McKechnie. They all gave selflessly of their time. In terms of accuracy of content (and especially in terms of the hunting community at large), I owe a great debt to Oliver Braid.

I owe everything else to my partner, Magda, my daughters, Shelby and Dylan, and my parents, without whose encouragement (and patience) I'd be a lesser version of myself.

NOTES

1

1. National Police Chiefs' Council (NPCC), *Online CSA Activist Groups: National Annual Threat Assessment*, May 2023.
2. Article 24a states that:

   (1) A person other than a constable may arrest without a warrant –
       (a) anyone who is in the act of committing an indictable offence;
       (b) anyone whom he has reasonable grounds for suspecting to be committing an indictable offence.

   (2) Where an indictable offence has been committed, a person other than a constable may arrest without a warrant –
       (a) anyone who is guilty of the offence;
       (b) anyone whom he has reasonable grounds for suspecting to be guilty of it.

   (3) But the power of summary arrest conferred by subsection (1) or (2) is exercisable only if –
       (a) the person making the arrest has reasonable grounds for believing that for any of the reasons mentioned in subsection (4) it is necessary to arrest the person in question; and
       (b) it appears to the person making the arrest that it is not reasonably practicable for a constable to make it instead.

   (4) The reasons are to prevent the person in question –
       (a) causing physical injury to himself or any other person;
       (b) suffering physical injury;
       (c) causing loss of or damage to property; or
       (d) making off before a constable can assume responsibility for him.

3. www.bbc.co.uk/news/uk-england-london-45811339

2

1. National Society for the Prevention of Cruelty to Children (NSPCC), 'Child sexual offences jump 57% in 5 years', *News*, 8 Oct. 2020. www.nspcc.org

.uk/about-us/news-opinion/2020/child-sexual-offences-rise/ (accessed 26 Nov. 2020).

2. US Department of Health and Human Services, *Child maltreatment*, 2018. www.acf.hhs.gov/sites/default/files/cb/cm2018.pdf (accessed 8 Oct. 2020).

3. www.nationalcrimeagency.gov.uk/news/nca-leads-international-coali tion-tackling-child-sexual-abuse

4. The Office for National Statistics (ONS) puts the number of those having experienced sexual abuse before turning 16 at 3.1 million in a population of 67 million, or at roughly 5 per cent (*The Report of the Independent Inquiry into Child Sexual Abuse*, Oct. 2022).

5. It is likely that the sexual abuse of males is underreported. See also C. McNaughton Nicholls, S. Scott and L. Kelly, '"The biggest problem for me, I think, was nobody asked me." Why asking about abuse matters to service users: Findings from an evaluation of routine enquiry in Adult Mental Health Services in England: Carol McNaughton Nicholls', *European Journal of Public Health*, 24 (2014), issue suppl. 2; H. Beckett, D. Holmes and J. Walker, *Child sexual exploitation: Definition & guide for professionals: Extended text* (University of Bedfordshire, 2017); D. Allnock and R. Atkinson, '"Snitches get stitches": School-specific barriers to victim disclosure and peer reporting of sexual harm committed by young people in school contexts', *Child Abuse & Neglect*, 89 (2019), 7–17.

6. *The Report of the Independent Inquiry into Child Sexual Abuse*, Oct. 2022, p. 3.

7. Home Office, *Group-based characteristics of child sexual exploitation*, Dec. 2020, https://assets.publishing.service.gov.uk/government/uploads/system/uploads/attachment_data/file/944206/Group-based_CSE_Paper.pdf

8. A. Zabin, *Conversations with a paedophile: Inside the mind of a sexual predator* (Fort Lee, NJ: Barricade Books, 2013), p. xi.

9. H. A. Turner, D. Finkelhor and R. Ormrod, 'Poly-victimization in a national sample of children and youth', *American Journal of Preventive Medicine*, 38(3) (2010), 323–30.

10. A. J. Sedlak, J. Mettenburg, M. Basena, I. Peta, K. McPherson, A. Greene and S. Li, *Fourth national incidence study of child abuse and neglect (NIS-4)* (Washington, DC: US Department of Health and Human Services, 2010), p. 9.

11. Turner, Finkelhor and Ormrod, 'Poly-victimization'.

12. The report relied on evidence provided by the National Child Abuse and Neglect Data System and the Annual Fifty State Survey conducted by Prevent Child Abuse America.

13. According to Radford Benjamin of the *Skeptical Inquirer*, as reported by D. McCollam in 'The shame game', *Columbia Journalism Review*, 45(5) (2007), 28–33, https://archives.cjr.org/feature/the_shame_game.php

14. It may well be that law enforcement has been effective in reducing the numbers. For example, in September 1994, the FBI opened a new case that came to be called *Operation Innocent Images*, and more agents and support staff were called in, including to pose as children to bait predators. Also, in 1996, Megan's Law (US) came into effect, mandating public

disclosure of information about registered sex offenders, when required, to protect the public. That same year, the Internet Watch Foundation set up a hotline to promote the reporting of online child sexual abuse imagery. A year later, the UK Parliament passed the Sex Offenders Act 1997 (c. 51), which made various sex offenders (defined as anyone who has been convicted of sexual offences) subject to notification requirements, thereby implementing a sex offenders registry.

15. www.ojp.gov/pdffiles1/ojjdp/184741.pdf

16. *The Report of the Independent Inquiry into Child Sexual Abuse*, Oct. 2022, pp. 43, 47.

17. Internet Watch Foundation.

18. *The Report of the Independent Inquiry into Child Sexual Abuse*, Oct. 2022, p. 3; see also www.gov.uk/government/publications/the-economic-and-social-cost-of-contact-child-sexual-abuse/ (accessed 25 Nov. 2022).

19. The estimated average lifetime cost per victim of nonfatal child maltreatment is $210,012 in 2010 dollars, including $32,648 in childhood health care costs; $10,530 in adult medical costs; $144,360 in productivity losses; $7,728 in child welfare costs; $6,747 in criminal justice costs; and $7,999 in special education costs. The estimated average lifetime cost per death is $1,272,900, including $14,100 in medical costs and $1,258,800 in productivity losses. The total lifetime economic burden resulting from new cases of fatal and nonfatal child maltreatment in the United States in 2008 was approximately $124 billion. In sensitivity analysis, the total burden is estimated to be as large as $585 billion (X. Fang, D. S. Brown, C. S. Florence and J. A. Mercy, 'The economic burden of child maltreatment in the United States and implications for prevention', *Child Abuse & Neglect*, 36(2) (2012), 156–65).

20. www.childfund.org/uploadedFiles/public_site/media/ODI%20Report%20%20The%20cost%20and%20economic%20impact%20of%20violence%20against%20children.pdf (accessed 25 Nov. 2022).

21. Widely reported recent cases in the US include those of college football coach Jerry Sandusky and US gymnastics doctor Larry Nassar.

22. J. Evans, 'Vigilance and vigilantes: Thinking psychoanalytically about anti-paedophile action', *Theoretical Criminology*, 7 (2003), 163–89.

23. J. Farrell, 'Perverted justice: An exploration of the origins, operations and future of paedophile hunting in the UK', unpublished master's dissertation, Universiteit Utrecht, 2018.

24. D. Pilgrim, 'Child sexual abuse, moral panics and emancipatory practice', *Critical and Radical Social Work*, 5 (2017), 7–22.

25. C. Ingraham and J. Reeves , 'New media, new panics', in P. Decherney and K. Sender (eds.), *Stuart Hall lives: Cultural studies in an age of digital media* (Abingdon: Routledge, 2016), pp. 455–67, p. 456.

26. J. Urry, 'Globalization and citizenship', *Journal of World-Systems Research*, 5 (1999), 310–24, p. 320.

27. There were also several precursors in the UK that helped build a certain atmosphere that promoted citizen involvement in catching suspected paedophiles. For example, the murder of Sarah Payne led to *News of the*

World's name-and-shame campaign (www.theguardian.com/society/2000/aug/04/childprotection). The Paulsgrove Riots ('Residents Against Paedophiles') were a consequence of this campaign and included a vigilante attack against a paediatrician by those unable to distinguish between paedophile and paediatrician (www.theguardian.com/uk/2000/aug/30/childprotection.society). Then there was a collaboration between a former CSE victim and a journalist (Shy Keenan and Sarah Macdonald) to catch Shy's childhood abuser admitting his abuse on secret camera footage and expose it on *Newsnight* (http://news.bbc.co.uk/1/hi/england/1849748.stm). Moreover, in 2002, the BBC aired a documentary called *The Hunt for Britain's Paedophiles* (http://news.bbc.co.uk/1/hi/uk/2027864.stm), which may have led Pete Townsend to use the vigilante defence in court when charged with possession of CSE imagery. In 2005, Scotland Yard began using decoys to bait predators.

28. https://archives.cjr.org/feature/the_shame_game.php?page=all
29. E. Chiang and T. Grant , 'Deceptive identity performance: Offender moves and multiple identities in online child abuse conversations', *Applied Linguistics*, 40 (2019), 675–98.
30. All excerpts taken from McCollam, 'The shame game'.
31. Luke Dittrich, 'Tonight on "Dateline" this man will die', *Esquire*, 5 Sept. 2007, http://esquire.com/features/predator0907
32. McCollam, 'The shame game'.
33. McCollam, 'The shame game'.
34. www.theguardian.com/culture/2008/may/31/features16.theguide6 (accessed 25 Jan. 2023).
35. www.theguardian.com/culture/2008/may/31/features16.theguide6 (accessed 25 Jan. 2023).
36. The teams that followed the documentary partly developed out of a critique of Stinson, who was known to take donations. After the documentary, a funding page was set up that quickly attracted about £30,000 in donations. No one seems to know what happened to the money (www.coventrytelegraph.net/news/local-news/stinson-hunter-plans-vanish-after-9655098). This is almost certainly where the voluntary orientation of hunting stems from. Additionally, Stinson used a large camera to record the evidence and sent it through to the police. In some instances, he says he just did the recording and let the suspects walk away. This is possibly why there is now such a focus on recording the arrest. There is some debate around the origins of the first live-streamed sting. Some people say it was Shane Brannigan, who used it when his video camera battery died; other people suspect it was Julie of Internet Interceptors. Both of these characters are key to the type of hunting we see today.
37. National Police Chiefs' Council (NPCC), *Online CSA Activist Group (OCAG) activity across the United Kingdom: Interim figures* (2019), internal publication, used with permission. These figures decreased between April 2020 and March 2021 to 145 hunting groups and 1,148 incidents (according to an update produced by the NPCC dated August 2021).

38. NPCC, *Online CSA Activist Group (OCAG) activity across the United Kingdom*, Aug. 2021, used with permission.

39. National Crime Agency (NCA) / National Assessments Centre (NAC), *Public activism against suspected child abusers*, Intelligence Assessment, NAC (18)028, Dec. 2018.

40. NCA/NAC, *Public activism against suspected child abusers*.

41. The percentages for April 2020 to March 2021 were London 14.1 per cent with the West Midlands 13.7 per cent, Yorkshire & the Humber 12.3 per cent and the East Midlands 12.2 per cent.

42. These are the percentages for the April 2022 to March 2023 period. In previous years, the percentages were closer to 50 per cent in each case. It is not clear why 'door knocks' have increased in popularity.

43. NCA/NAC, *Public activism against suspected child abusers*. Of the 191 teams in 2019, 84 are known to have collaborated with another team on at least one sting (NPCC assessment).

44. NCA/NAC, *Public activism against suspected child abusers*.

45. K. Rickard and K. M. Bakke, 'Legacies of wartime order: Punishment attacks and social control in Northern Ireland', *Security Studies*, 30(4) (2021), 603–36.

46. National Police Chiefs' Council (NPCC), *Online CSA Activist Groups: National Annual Threat Assessment*, May 2023.

47. This suspicion is shared by the NCA in warning that there aren't likely to be good protective measures to prevent inaccurate and/or malicious entries. See NCA/NAC, *Public activism against suspected child abusers*.

48. https://offenders.org.uk

49. www.bbc.co.uk/news/uk-england-50302912 (accessed 8 Oct. 2020).

50. NCA/NAC, *Public activism against suspected child abusers*. By their own admission, the data is patchy.

51. NPCC, *Threat Assessment*, May 2023. A caveat to bear in mind is that this percentage is based on only 33 per cent of all recorded incidents for the April 2022 to March 2023 period.

52. HM Government, 2021.

53. *Stop It Now*: www.stopitnow.org.uk/concerned-about-your-own-thoughts-or-behaviour/concerned-about-use-of-the-internet/get-the-facts/consequences/being-on-the-sex-offenders-register-sor/ (accessed 5 Dec. 2022). Before this legal change, Section 15a of the 2003 Sexual Offences Act made it a criminal offence to arrange to meet a child under 16 for a sexual purpose, whether for oneself or someone else; an offence which carried a maximum sentence of ten years' imprisonment and automatic barring from working with children or vulnerable adults.

54. *Stop It Now*.

55. It is widely believed that advances in AI will worsen child sexual abuse (www.theguardian.com/society/2023/jul/18/ai-could-worsen-epidemic-of-child-sexual-abuse-warns-uk-agency).

56. The Sex Offenders Register has been in operation since the Sex Offences Act of 1997.

57. *Stop It Now*.

58. Chief Constable Simon Bailey, as quoted on *Stop It Now* website.

59. The most important of these regulations fall under the Regulation of Investigative Powers Act (RIPA) 2000.
60. NPCC, *Online CSA Activist Group (OCAG) activity across the United Kingdom*, Aug. 2021, used with permission.
61. NCA/NAC, *Public activism against suspected child abusers*.

3

1. As the Wetherspoons chain of pubs is affectionately known.

4

1. https://shaunattwood.com/scotlands-wolf-pack-hunter-gordon-buchan-true-crime-podcast-203/
2. It may well be that this trend towards professionalism was seen as a criticism of their 'unprofessionalism' by the older guard, some of whom responded by, for example, using a 'nonce bingo' card for stings. From this point there is a marked interest from teams to either thematise and justify their 'unprofessionalism' or to perform their 'professionalism'.
3. He spoke through his solicitor, as reported in *The Courier*, 18 June 2021 (www.thecourier.co.uk/fp/news/courts/2316367/a-bunch-of-thugs-vigi lante-denounces-wolf-pack-paedophile-hunters-after-chaotic-angus-pro test/).
4. www.theguardian.com/society/2019/aug/06/scotlands-child-abuse-activ ists-we-embrace-the-vigilante-label
5. www.thescottishsun.co.uk/news/4793964/wolf-pack-hunters-stuart-mcin roy-edinburgh/. A Glasgow kiss is a euphemism for a headbutt.
6. C. Brettell, *When they read what we write: The politics of ethnography* (Granby, MA: Bergin & Garvey, 1996), p. 14.
7. Brettell, *When they read what we write*, p. 13.
8. H. Shapira, *Waiting for José: The minutemen's pursuit of America* (Princeton, NJ: Princeton University Press, 2013), p. 12.
9. www.theatlantic.com/ideas/archive/2023/08/buckley-new-york-private-schools-wealth-inequality/675066/?utm_source=newsletter&utm_ medium=email&utm_campaign=one-story-to-read-today&utm_ content=20230822&utm_term=One+Story+to+Read+Today
10. Most hunters and decoys choose a 'last name' that reflects their role. I chose 'Lenz' to indicate that I was an 'outsider' and also a foreigner, in a subculture dominated by the white British working class. That way, I figured, people would have reason to know there was an outside observer in their midst.

5

1. I know of teams, though Jay's isn't one of them, who use a smartphone app designed for use by police but easily and freely available to remind

themselves of what counts as an offence and what needs to be proven to warrant a charge by police. The name of the app is Pocket Sergeant.

6

1. For the NCA, 'activists confronting suspects themselves rather than simply passing the suspect's details to the police is not an activity that in any way contributes to the protection of children'. They go on to say that 'this raises the question of whether this ... is motivated by ... personal gratification or a sense of self-worth or self-importance' (National Crime Agency (NCA) / National Assessments Centre (NAC), *Public activism against suspected child abusers*, Intelligence Assessment, NAC (18)028, Dec. 2018).
2. Partial transcript from a sting.
3. And it is why, in a 2019 BBC interview, the National Police Chiefs' Council lead for child sexual abuse activism said, 'When these groups say that they are acting in the interests of children, largely they are acting in their own interests, their self-aggrandisement and their desire to exercise force against so-called perpetrators of child abuse' ('Police concerns over rise of "paedophile hunters"', *BBC News*, 6 Nov. 2019, www.bbc.co.uk/news/uk-england-50302912).
4. P. M. Campbell, 'Interactive fiction and narrative theory: Towards an anti-theory', *New England Review and Bread Loaf Quarterly*, 10 (1987), 76–84.
5. C. Booker, *The seven basic plots: Why we tell stories* (London: Continuum, 2004), p. 33.
6. Booker, *The seven basic plots*, p. 33.
7. B. Bettelheim, *The uses of enchantment: The meaning and importance of fairy tales* (London: Penguin Books, 1991), p. 8. I accept that this may be true of 'Disney-fied' fairy tales more than original ones.
8. C. Vogler, *The writer's journey* (Studio City, CA: Michael Wiese Productions, 2007), p. 114; Bettelheim, *The uses of enchantment*.
9. A. Tippett, 'The rise of paedophile hunters: To what extent are cyber-vigilante groups a productive form of policing, retribution and justice?' *Criminology & Criminal Justice* (2022), https://doi.org/10.1177/17488958221136845
10. K. Richards, 'Born this way? A qualitative examination of public perceptions of the causes of pedophilia and sexual offending against children', *Deviant Behavior*, 39(7) (2018), 835–51.
11. The precise number was 94,342; see www.stopitnow.org.uk
12. www.stopitnow.org.uk
13. Tippett, 'The rise of paedophile hunters'.
14. Tippett, 'The rise of paedophile hunters'.
15. 'Police concerns over rise of "paedophile hunters"', *BBC News*, 6 Nov. 2019.

7

1. A. Zabin, *Conversations with a pedophile: Inside the mind of a sexual predator* (Fort Lee, NJ: Barricade Books, 2013), p. 73.
2. Zabin, *Conversations with a pedophile*, pp. 109–10.
3. Zabin, *Conversations with a pedophile*, p. 97.
4. Zabin, *Conversations with a pedophile*, p. xi.
5. Zabin *Conversations with a pedophile*, p. x.
6. Some 85 per cent of predators self-identified as white (with only 10 per cent identifying as Asian: www.theguardian.com/politics/2020/dec/15/child-sex ual-abuse-gangs-white-men-home-office-report; National Police Chiefs' Council (NPCC), *Online CSA Activist Groups: National Annual Threat Assessment*, May 2023. There's a big caveat in that only 69.2 per cent of all recorded incidents recorded the ethnicity of the suspect. See also: https:// fullfact.org/crime/what-do-we-know-about-ethnicity-people-involved-sex ual-offences-against-children/
7. Home Office, *Group-based child sexual exploitation*, 2020, https://assets .publishing.service.gov.uk/government/uploads/system/uploads/attach ment_data/file/944206/Group-based_CSE_Paper.pdf
8. G. Perrotta , 'Pedophilia: Definition, classifications, criminological and neurobiological profiles, and clinical treatments. A complete review', *Open Journal of Pediatrics and Child Health*, 5(1) (2020), 019–026.
9. www.independent.co.uk/voices/newcastle-grooming-scandal-exploit ation-victims-sarah-champion-race-a7890106.html
10. Perrotta, 'Pedophilia'.
11. Online paedophiles are estimated to be between 18 and 25 years old on average, based on a meta-review in 2011; see K. M. Babchishin, R. K. Hanson and C. A. Hermann, 'The characteristics of online sex offenders: A meta-analysis', *Sexual Abuse*, 23(1) (2011), 92–123. The average age of 39 is based on more recent UK police arrest data from 2019. The difference in age could mean that today's online offenders are, on average, older or that UK online offenders are older than those in the US (where most of the studies reviewed in the meta-review were based).
12. J. Neutze, M. C. Seto, G. A. Schaefer, I. A. Mundt and K. M. Beier, 'Predictors of child pornography offenses and child sexual abuse in a community sample of paedophiles and hebephiles', *Sexual Abuse*, 23(2) (2011), 212–42.
13. NPCC, *Threat Assessment*, May 2023.
14. Babchishin, Hanson and Hermann, 'The characteristics of online sex offenders'.

8

1. H. Shapira, *Waiting for José: The minutemen's pursuit of America* (Princeton, NJ: Princeton University Press, 2013), p. 132.

2. Police prioritise targets using the Kent Internet Risk Assessment Tool (KIRAT), one of the criteria of which is the risk predators pose to real children. For more details: www.rma.scot/wp-content/uploads/2023/01/Kent-Internet-Risk-Assessment-Tool-2-KIRAT-2.pdf

3. These six points are contained in the paper presented to VPP 06/06/18 and the National Police Chiefs' Council thereafter.

4. E. Hobsbawm, *Bandits*, new edition (London: Abacus, 2001), p. 20.

5. Hobsbawm, *Bandits*, pp. 29–30.

6. Hobsbawm, *Bandits*, p. 49.

7. G. Weston, 'Superheroes and comic-book vigilantes versus real-life vigilantes: An anthropological answer to the Kick-Ass paradox', *Journal of Graphic Novels and Comics*, 4(2) (2013), 223–34.

8. A. Blok, 'The peasant and the brigand: Social bandits reconsidered', *Comparative Studies in Society and History*, 14(4) (1972), 494–503.

9. P. Sant Cassia, 'Banditry, myth, and terror in Cyprus and other Mediterranean societies', *Comparative Studies in Society and History*, 35 (4) (1993), 773–95.

10. R. Abrahams, *Vigilant citizens: Vigilantism and the state* (Cambridge: Polity Press, 1998), p. 164 (paraphrased).

11. Baroness Casey's report was published in March 2023.

12. www.bbc.com/news/world-europe-46207304

9

1. J. Malcolm, *The journalist and the murderer* (London: Granta Books, 2011), p. 1.

2. W. F. Whyte, *Street corner society: The social structure of an Italian slum*, 4th edition (Chicago, IL: University of Chicago Press. 2012), p. 347.

3. D. P. Warwick, 'Tearoom trade: Means and ends in social research', *The Hastings Center Studies*, 1(1) (1973), 27–38, cited in L. Humphreys, *Tearoom trade, enlarged edition: Impersonal sex in public places* (Piscataway, NJ: Transaction Publishers, 1975), p. 211.

4. This sting is reminiscent of a classic hunting mantra spoken to suspects: 'If it was my child, I wouldn't be here with a camera, I'd be here with a shovel.' The language of stings is very often made up of stock phrases, like memes. Teams are conscious of working within a cultural movement and reusing these established parts of the culture. This leads to a loss of the immediatism of hunting as a practice. Just like paedophiles always come up with the same limited excuses, teams have a similar limited number of responses/interjections. These provide a chance for new teams to 'walk in the footsteps of giants', that is, by repeating the words they've already heard other more established teams uttering. It also means no team runs the risk of doing something original that could be criticised as unprofessional or glory hunting.

10

1. Edited extract from T. Jones, *Ultra: The underworld of Italian football* (London: Head of Zeus, 2019), in *The Observer*, 15 Sept. 2019, 'The New Review', p. 13.

11

1. © X Corp. Full details: Copyright 2024 X Corp and other contributors. Code licensed under the MIT Licence: http://opensource.org/licenses/MIT. Graphics licensed under CC-BY 4.0: https://creativecommons.org/licenses /by/4.0/
2. Even if 'only' 2,000 to 4,000 people may watch a sting as it unfolds live, as many as 250,000 others may have seen the sting within days of it being posted online.

12

1. The specific way in which stings are conducted serves to confirm some of their core beliefs, specifically in relation to both the animalistic nature of their target as well as belief in the absolute certainty of his guilt. Hunters will closely surround predators, ostensibly to discourage them from escaping, but in doing so create the impression of a caged animal. While reactions of predators vary, many can be seen to cower under the weight of the confrontation, trapped and struggling to explain themselves in response to a recurrent question: '*Why?!*' Thus, they end up physically embodying their alleged guilt for the world to see live online. Certainty of their guilt is further reinforced when hunters manage to get the predator to admit to the charges, and to knowingly committing an offence. That such admissions are often made under some duress is, for hunters, neither here nor there.
2. There are those who suggest that 'vigilantism' is a political act through which those rendered voiceless by the democratic state can critique its claim to a rule of law (e.g., D. M. Goldstein, '"In our own hands": Lynching, justice, and the law in Bolivia', *American Ethnologist*, *30* (2003), 22–43). Others have theorised violent vigilantism as a collective ritual performance that reinforces the unity of a moral group identity (e.g., M. Asif and D. Weenink, 'Vigilante rituals theory: A cultural explanation of vigilante violence', *European Journal of Criminology*, *19*(2) (2019), 1–20), even though most teams make sure to avoid violence so as not to be labelled vigilantes. And there are those who argue that those who are predisposed to authoritarianism and moral certainty are especially likely to administer unauthorised punishment to deviants (e.g., K. A. DeCelles and K. Aquino, 'Dark knights: When and why an employee becomes a workplace vigilante', *Academy of Management Review*, *45* (2020), 528–48), and while there may be merit in this assertion, the social-psychological models on which these

assertions typically rely tend to neglect to consider the role of lived experience as integral to the dynamic complexity of the motives and emotions involved (e.g., J. Van Stekelenburg and B. Klandermans, 'Individuals in movements: A social psychology of contention', in C. Roggeband and B. Klandermans (eds.), *Handbook of social movements across disciplines* (Cham, Switzerland: Springer, 2017)), pp. 103–39.

3. Despite a growing interest in citizen activism more broadly, research to date has not really offered all that much insight into the lifeworld of hunting teams as a resource for better understanding why they persist with extreme methods. While researchers across such varied fields as political science (R. Dudai, 'Entryism, mimicry and victimhood work: The adoption of human rights discourse by right-wing groups in Israel', *International Journal of Human Rights*, 21 (2017), 866–88; G. Super, 'Volatile sovereignty: Governing crime through the community in Khayelitsha', *Law & Society Review*, 50 (2016), 450–83), criminology (L. Johnston, 'What is vigilantism?', *British Journal of Criminology*, 36 (1996), 220–36; P. H. Robinson and S. M. Robinson, *Shadow vigilantes: How distrust in the justice system breeds a new kind of lawlessness* (Amherst, NY: Prometheus Books, 2018)), journalism (e.g., W. E. Burrows, *Vigilante!* (New York: Harcourt Brace Jovanovich, 1976)), history (e.g., E. Hobsbawm, *Bandits*, new edition (London: Abacus, 2001)) and organisation theory (e.g., B. Crawford and M. T. Dacin, 'Policing work: Emotions and violence in institutional work', *Organization Studies*, 42 (2020), 1–22; B. Crawford and M. T. Dacin, 'Punishment and institutions: A macrofoundations perspective', in C. Steele, T. Hannigan, V. Glaser, M. Toubiana and J. Gehman (eds.), *Macrofoundations: Exploring the institutionally situated nature of activity* (Bingley: Emerald Publishing, 2021), pp. 97–119) have offered significant insight into the contextual conditions for vigilantism, the experience of being a vigilante has been largely neglected (cf. R. Bateson , 'The politics of vigilantism', *Comparative Political Studies*, 54 (2020), 923–55). Social psychological models of their deeper motivations tend to essentialise vigilantes through the hypothetical attribution of individual psychological characteristics that predispose them to punitive violence. Others have focused on the legality of live streaming, particularly as relates to human rights and the rights to privacy (J. Purshouse, '"Paedophile hunter": Criminal procedure, and fundamental human rights', *Journal of Law and Society*, 47 (2020), 384–411). Linguistic analyses of chat logs have shown that adult decoys posing as children tend to sustain interactions with suspected predators past the point where a real child would have likely ceased communication (E. Chiang and T. Grant, 'Deceptive identity performance: Offender moves and multiple identities in online child abuse conversations', *Applied Linguistics*, 40 (2019), 675–98). These differences in online behaviour raise concerns around entrapment in a factual, if not strictly legal, sense. Legally, Section 67 of the UK's Serious Crime Act of 2015 has made (online) sexual communication with a child a criminal offence that carries a maximum two-year prison sentence, regardless of whether the child is simulated or real. Other research has placed paedophile hunting in the broader context of websleuthing (E. Yardley, A. G. T. Lynes, D. Wilson and E. Kelly, 'What's the deal with "websleuthing"? News media representations of amateur

detectives in networked spaces', *Crime, Media, Culture*, *14*(1) (2018), 81–109), highlighting common motivating factors such as, for example, a desire to prevent others from victimisation, infotainment witnessing, wound culture, naming and shaming suspects, and justice or closure.

13

1. www.cambridge-news.co.uk/news/cambridge-news/cambridgeshire-police-sex-assault-dropped-14685485

14

1. Quoted from, J. Freedland, 'Why lies spread faster than facts', *The Guardian*, 8 March 2019, www.theguardian.com/books/2019/mar/08/anti-vaxxers-the-momo-challenge-why-lies-spread-faster-than-facts
2. To stave off concerns about the harm inflicted on family members, hunters typically shun responsibility (e.g., 'none of this would have happened if he hadn't been talking to kids') or will invoke the 'greater good' argument (e.g., to get a predator off the streets is ultimately what matters). This is clearly illustrated in the vignette in which COBRA refuses to take accountability for the harm that their video was doing to the predator's family. Albert Bandura directly linked such disregard for injurious effects on third parties, in addition to the displacement of responsibility and the dehumanisation of the recipients of maltreatment, to moral disengagement (A. Bandura, 'Moral disengagement in the perpetration of inhumanities', *Personality and Social Psychology Review*, *3* (1999), 193–209; 'Selective moral disengagement in the exercise of moral agency', *Journal of Moral Education*, *31* (2002), 101–19). Moreover, hunters typically deflect police criticisms through a mix of conspiracy thinking, e.g., 'authority doesn't care because there's no money in it for them', and dismissing police allegations of their narcissistic motives by using such suspicions as proof that the police have no idea what they are talking about. Similarly, critical coverage in the media is dismissed as extremely biased 'fake news'.
3. G. Marinovich and J. Silva, *The Bang-Bang Club, movie tie-in: Snapshots from a hidden war* (London: Basic Books, 2011).

16

1. Jonathan Barton was acquitted of all charges on 6 December 2023. As reported by ITV (who first publicised the case), Barton, 41, faced eight charges against eight different women during a trial at Dumbarton Sheriff Court. Six alleged sexual assault by touching during ballet classes. Two alleged 'abuse of position of trust' relating to sexual relationships. Barton said he had sex with both girls but insisted they were over the age of 18. The charges ranged from 2004 until 2019 (www.itv.com/news/2023-12-06/scottish-ballet-teacher-acquitted-of-sexual-assaults-on-teenage-pupils).

18

1. https://en.wikipedia.org/wiki/Operation_Ore

19

1. This concluding chapter relies in part on something I wrote in the conclusion to M. de Rond, J. Lok and A. Marrison, 'To catch a predator: The lived experience of extreme practices', *Academy of Management Journal*, 65(3) (2022), 870–902.
2. The poll is available here: www.prri.org/research/qanon-conspiracy-ameri can-politics-report/
3. According to Bobby Jones from the PRRI: www.nytimes.com/2021/05/27 /us/politics/qanon-republicans-trump.html
4. G. Volpicelli, 'How QAnon took hold in the UK', *Wired*, 21 Sept. 2020, www.wired.co.uk/article/qanon-uk (accessed 4 Oct. 2020).
5. Hiram Edson, manuscript fragment on his 'Life and experience', n.d., Ellen G. White Research Center, James White Library, Andrews University, Berrien Springs, MI, pp. 4–5; and F. D. Nichol, *The Midnight Cry* (Hagerstown, MD: Review and Herald Publishing Association, 1945), p. 458.
6. www.theatlantic.com/magazine/archive/2023/03/tv-politics-entertain ment-metaverse/672773/
7. www.washingtonpost.com/opinions/crises-and-the-collectivist-tempta tion/2020/04/02/751241b8-74fa-11ea-87da-77a8136c1a6d_story.html
8. E. Hoffer, *The true believer: Thoughts on the nature of mass movements* (New York: Harper, 1951).
9. www.theatlantic.com/magazine/archive/2023/03/tv-politics-entertain ment-metaverse/672773/
10. S. Pinker, 'Reason to believe: How and why irrationality takes hold, and what do to about it', *Persuasion*, 9 Jan. 2023, www.persuasion.commu nity/p/steven-pinker-reason-to-believe?utm_source=substack&utm_ medium=email
11. K. M. Douglas, J. E. Uscinski, R. M. Sutton, A. Cichocka, T. Nefes, C. S. Ang and F. Deravi, 'Understanding conspiracy theories', *Political Psychology*, 40 (2019), 3–35, p. 8.
12. J. A. Whitson and A. D. Galinsky, 'Lacking control increases illusory pattern perception', *Science*, 322(5898) (2008), 115–17, as cited by Ellen Cushing in *The Atlantic*, May 2020: www.theatlantic.com/ideas/archive /2020/05/i-was-a-teenage-conspiracist/610975/
13. Whitson and Galinsky, 'Lacking control'.
14. See A. Cichocka, M. Marchlewska and A. G. De Zavala, 'Does self-love or self-hate predict conspiracy beliefs? Narcissism, self-esteem, and the endorsement of conspiracy theories', *Social Psychological and Personality Science*, 7(2) (2016), 157–66; R. Imhoff and P. K. Lamberty, 'Too special to be duped: Need for uniqueness motivates conspiracy beliefs', *European Journal of Social Psychology*, 47(6) (2017), 724–34; A. Lantian, D. Muller,

C. Nurra and K. M. Douglas , 'I know things they don't know!', *Social Psychology*, *48*(3) (2017), 160–73; all cited by Ellen Cushing in *The Atlantic*, May 2020, www.theatlantic.com/ideas/archive/2020/05/i-was-a-teenage-conspiracist/610975/

15. Ellen Cushing in *The Atlantic*, May 2020, www.theatlantic.com/ideas/archive/2020/05/i-was-a-teenage-conspiracist/610975/

16. J. Byford, 'I've been talking to conspiracy theorists for 20 years – here are my six rules of engagement', *The Conversation*, 22 July 2020, https://theconversation.com

17. These are four of seven basic plots identified by C. Booker, *The seven basic plots: Why we tell stories* (London: Continuum, 2004).

18. T. Ingold, *Anthropology: Why it matters* (Cambridge: Polity Press, 2018), pp. 14–15.

Epilogue

1. H. S. Thompson, *Kingdom of fear: Loathsome secrets of a star-crossed child in the final days of the American century* (New York: Simon and Schuster, 2003).

2. Martin McDonagh, from *Three billboards outside Ebbing, Missouri*. Reprinted with permission.

Appendix: Notes on Methodology

1. This 'Methodological Note' relies heavily on an academic article reporting on the first three years of this fieldwork and published as M. de Rond, J. Lok and A. Marrison, 'To catch a predator: The lived experience of extreme practices', *Academy of Management Journal*, *65*(3) (2022), 870–902.

2. C. Geertz, 'Making experience, authoring selves', in V. W. Turner and E. Bruner (eds.), *The anthropology of experience* (Urbana, IL: University of Illinois Press, 1986), pp. 373–80, p. 373.

3. T. Ingold, *Anthropology: Why it matters* (Cambridge: Polity Press, 2018).

4. E. M. Bruner, 'Ethnography as narrative', in V. W. Turner and E. M. Bruner (eds.), *The anthropology of experience* (Urbana, IL: University of Illinois Press, 1986), pp. 139–55.

5. Geertz, 'Making experience, authoring selves', p. 375.

6. S. Mantere and M. Ketokivi , 'Reasoning in organization science', *Academy of Management Review*, *38* (2013), 70–89.

7. D. A. Gioia, K. G. Corley and A. L. Hamilton , 'Seeking qualitative rigor in inductive research: Notes on the Gioia methodology', *Organizational Research Methods*, *16* (2013), 15–31.

8. M. Ketokivi and S. Mantere, 'Two strategies for inductive reasoning in organizational research', *Academy of Management Review*, *35* (2010), 315–33.

9. M. Jackson, *Existential anthropology* (New York: Berghahn Books, 2008).

10. E.g., J. Schad, M. W. Lewis, S. Raisch and W. K. Smith, 'Paradox research in management science: Looking back to move forward', *Academy of Management Annals*, 10 (2016), 5–64.

11. N. Brunsson, *The organization of hypocrisy: Talk, decisions and actions in organizations* (Chichester: Wiley, 1989).

12. T. R. Schatzki, *The site of the social: A philosophical account of the constitution of social life and change* (University Park, PA: Penn State Press, 2002).

13. A. Carlsen, 'After James on identity', in P. Adler (ed.), *The Oxford handbook of sociology and organization studies: Classical foundations* (Oxford: Oxford University Press, 200), pp. 421–43; A. Carlsen, 'On the tacit side of organizational identity: Narrative unconscious and figured practice', *Culture and Organization*, 22 (2016), 107–35.

14. C. Booker, *The seven basic plots: Why we tell stories* (London: Continuum, 2004); J. Campbell and B. Moyers, *The power of myth* (New York: Anchor, 2011).

15. B. E. Ashforth and G. E. Kreiner, 'How can you do it?': Dirty work and the challenge of constructing a positive identity', *Academy of Management Review*, 24 (1999), 413–34; B. E. Ashforth, G. E. Kreiner, M. Clark and M. Fugate, 'Normalizing dirty work: Managerial tactics for countering occupational taint', *Academy of Management Journal*, 50 (2007), 149–74.

16. H. J. Rosenbaum and P. C. Sederberg, 'Vigilantism: An analysis of establishment violence', *Comparative Politics*, 6 (1974), 541–70; L. Johnston, 'What is vigilantism?', *British Journal of Criminology*, 36 (1996), 220–36.

17. N. Haslam and S. Loughnan, 'Dehumanization and infrahumanization', *Annual Review of Psychology*, 65 (2014), 399–423; G. T. Viki, I. Fullerton, H. Raggett, F. Tait and S. Wiltshire, 'The role of dehumanization in attitudes toward the social exclusion and rehabilitation of sex offenders', *Journal of Applied Social Psychology*, 42(10) (2012), 2349–67.

18. Bruner, 'Ethnography as narrative'.

19. Booker, *The seven basic plots*; J. S. Lawrence and R. Jewett, *The myth of the American superhero* (Grand Rapids, MI: Eerdmans, 2002).

20. A. Carlsen , 'On the tacit side of organizational identity: Narrative unconscious and figured practice', *Culture and Organization*, 22 (2016), 107–35; B. Czarniawska and C. Rhodes, 'Strong plots: Popular culture in management practice and theory', in P. Gagliardi and B. Czarniawska (eds.), *Management education and humanities* (Cheltenham: Edward Elgar, 2006), pp. 195–218.

21. Jackson, *Existential anthropology*.

22. R. May, *The cry for myth* (New York: W. W. Norton, 1991); I. McGregor, 'Zeal, identity, and meaning', in J. Greenberg, S. L. Koole and T. Pyszczynski (eds.), *Handbook of experimental existential psychology* (New York: Guilford Press, 2004), pp. 182–99.

When They Read What We Write

1. www.theage.com.au/national/victoria/government-may-amend-anti-vilifi cation-laws-after-neo-nazis-salute-on-spring-street-20230319-p5ctbm .html (accessed 28 March 2024).
2. P. Baker, *Outrageous: The story of Section 28 and Britain's battle for LGBT education* (London: Reaktion Books, 2022), p. 114.
3. https://cathyfox.wordpress.com/wp-content/uploads/2015/07/42-50nonces .jpg (accessed 28 March 2024).
4. M. Gaskill, *Witchfinders: A seventeenth-century English tragedy* (London: John Murray, 2005), pp. 9–33.
5. C. Bishop, 'Antagonism and relational aesthetics', *October, 110* (2004), 51–79.
6. E. Laclau and C. Mouffe, *Hegemony and socialist strategy: Towards a radical democratic politics* (London: Verso, 1985).
7. www.youtube.com/watch?v=vRBsaJPkt2Q (01:14:02) (accessed 28 March 2024).
8. www.channel4.com/news/gay-russian-sochi-hunting-season-we-are-the-hunted (accessed 28 March 2024).
9. https://cyberdisobedience.substack.com/p/putin-ukraine-nazis (accessed 28 March 2024).
10. www.washingtonpost.com/technology/2022/09/02/lgbtq-threats-hos pitals-libs-of-tiktok/ (accessed 28 March 2024).
11. www.youtube.com/watch?v=UwFhZMjOVtY (02:06:20) (accessed 28 March 2024).
12. www.youtube.com/watch?v=Sd6hXW6FN04 (00:13:05) (accessed 28 March 2024).
13. www.youtube.com/watch?v=JBy93QX7ysE&t=4816s (00:41:40) (accessed 28 March 2024).